Early reader response to

BUILD YOUR BUSINESS STRONGER—
AND DO IT QUICKLY!

A great work. As solid in concept and practice as is Ron's Lincoln-like value base. Loaded with guidelines, tips, and neat analogues that spell success at every turn.

> — **Hal Shook**, consultant in human resources, Author, *Flying Spirit: A Leader's Guide to Creating Great Organizations*

Concise, with easy-to-understand steps, Ron Guzik's ideas are practical and make it possible to quickly implement a plan of action geared toward the reader's own specific business. This book addresses the problems business owners constantly face.

> — **Annette Oliver**, Mesco-Oliver Group, Inc., Manufacturers' Representative

Ron's ideas have been instrumental in helping me to jump-start areas of my business that have been lacking, and to fine-tune my strong points. I found the marketing information especially helpful. The chapters are a quick read, but packed with information. All in all, I found this book to be very thorough, and it highlights the author's expertise in business start-ups and development. Thanks Ron!

> — **Sheila Lange**, Nationally Certified Massage Therapist, Ann Arbor, MI

A thoughtful and organized approach to building a business, starting with goal-setting for the entrepreneur, moving through planning the business, and culminating in honing the skills needed to survive and thrive in a new venture. The answer to the question posed by every aspiring business owner—namely, 'How do I get started?'—is to follow the systematic approach to building a business set forth in this book.

— **Robert F. Kemp, Esq.**, Kemp Law Offices, Chicago, IL

I am continually amazed, awed and inspired by Ron's ability to take the most complex business concepts and create a simple, manageable approach for even the "busiest" entrepreneur. I found myself looking forward to each new page that held for me wit & wisdom, ideas, strategies and common sense approaches that apply to my personal life as well as the life of my business. Reading Build your Business Stronger—And Do It Quickly was like having a conversation with a wise, experienced friend who cares as much about my individual success as he cares about the success of my business. Once again Ron has done the research to make my life easier. Thank you Ron for creating a way that I can grow my business and myself in the process.

— **Mary Elizabeth Murphy**, President, S.T.A.R. Resources, Charlotte, North Carolina

Ron's book opened my mind to new ideas about building my business, allowed me to see the important things in my life and helped me to bring together my business and my life.

— **Elida Hinojosa**, Estilos Salon, Joliet, IL

One of the most difficult journeys facing an individual in business is moving from employee to entrepreneur. Ron Guzik clears a seamless pathway from knowing yourself to creating your sales. Build Your Business Stronger—And Do It Quickly *is an invaluable tool for anyone conceiving or creating or running a business.*

— **Olivia McIvor**, Greenhouse Books,
Vancouver, BC, Canada

It's a known fact that most businesses fail within the first two years. I believe Ron's book would reduce that failure rate significantly. If an entrepreneur put as much effort into researching their business as Ron put into preparing his book, they would surely succeed.

— **Rich Behan, CPA**, Behan & Company, LTD.,
Carol Stream, IL

The lessons learned from this inspirational book by Ron Guzik are lessons that anyone can use as a blueprint for genuine business transformation. In his work and research Ron has complied a host of initiatives that entrepreneurs and businesses alike can use in response to challenges of an evolving business environment. Ron offers sound advice on how to sift through start-up issues and look into the future to build your business.

— **Sharon Haley**, Littleton, CO,
Professional Coach Personal/Business,
http://coaching4u.port5.com

Ron Guzik's book Build Your Business Stronger—And Do It Quickly *has great insight into developing the necessary personal motivation to create goals and a vision to make any entrepreneurial venture successful. He has also cap-tured a number of the most vital aspects of creating a rich and vibrant company culture. It is hands-on and easy to understand, a must read for all who have a small business or who are thinking of going into business for themselves.*

— **Anil Saxena**, organization development specialist, Chicago, IL

I found Ron Guzik's book to be very informative, and prac-tical on quite a range of business topics. I plan to keep the book within easy reach. It's such a wonderful reference resource.

— **Andrew L. Mace**, CPA,
William F. Gurrie & Co., LTD, Oak Brook, IL

Build your Business Stronger—And Do it Quickly *is a valu-able resource for any entrepreneur who wants to have the competitive edge in today's global market. The tools, strat-egies and methods discussed are worthwhile, easy to imple-ment and save time. Ronald Guzik's ideas for building a business are quick, while the end results for achieving suc-cess are long term.*

— **Christine Milostan**, CEO,
Milostan Creativity, Bloomingdale, IL,
milostancreativity.com

BUILD
YOUR BUSINESS
STRONGER
AND DO IT QUICKLY!

**Sales—Marketing—
Planning—Management—
Finance—and More!**

Ronald E. Guzik

Systems where People Matter

Also by the same author: *The Inner Game of Entrepreneuring*, 1999

Humanomics Publishing books are available at special discounts for bulk orders for training programs or as sales or other premiums. Please call 304-697-3236 or fax 304-697-3399.

ISBN 0-9666085-7-7

Library of Congress Control Number:

2002100254

Printed in Canada

First Edition

Editorial coordination: John Patrick Grace
Copy editing: Jennifer Adkins
Grace Associates/Editorial Consultants
P.O. Box 2395 • Huntington, West Virginia 25724

Cover and interior design: Mark S. Phillips,
Marketing+Design Group • www.marketingdesigngroup.com

Line drawings: Jan Dickinson

HUMANOMICS PUBLISHING
945 Fourth Avenue, Suite 200A • Huntington, WV 25701
Tel. (304) 697-3236 • E-Mail: publish@cloh.net

Distributed to the trade by:
Cumberland House Publishing
431 Harding Industrial Drive • Nashville, Tennessee 37211
Toll free – 888-439-BOOK (2665) • Fax (615) 832-0633
E-Mail: info@cumberlandhouse.com

The majority of chapters in this work originally were published as features in Svoboda's Business Magazine,which served Northern Illinois and Southern Wisconsin from 1993 to 2000.

CONTENTS

FOREWORD

This book by Ron Guzik is a must-have resource if you are committed to building a business. What I especially like about it is that you feel as if you are in a substantive conversation with someone who truly understands the positives and the challenges of managing and expanding a venture.

Many people have the idea that you develop an enterprise simply by plowing ahead, helter-skelter. *Build Your Business Stronger—And Do It Quickly* shows you there is considerable methodology and process to becoming a success.

One of the first ventures I ran was an antique center. My boss, the president of a $3 million mom and pop mall, asked me to build and manage an antique center connected to the property. I told him I had just started reading *Inc.*, the business magazine, and that they strongly encouraged entrepreneurs to write a business plan. My boss said business plans were for sissies. "Real entrepreneurs," he said, did it through gut instinct.

The company lost $250,000, and I lost my job. No one at all showed up to patronize the beautiful facility we had built.

As I write this, however, I have been involved in starting ventures for almost 20 years and have come a long way from the fiasco of the antique center in the mall. During the last two decades I have started a business incubator, the Penn State Technology Development Center; one of the largest trade associations in the world, The Eastern Technology Council; two online companies, BizLaunch (www.bizlaunch.net) and The ArtBiz (www.theartbiz.com); and a national newspaper, *Technology Times*. I have also run an Internet development firm, Mixed Media Work; a technology transfer center, and a marketing communications company.

I can assure you, therefore, that I have put myself into a position to appreciate the depth of the wisdom Ron Guzik conveys in this book.

Ron starts by challenging you to ask yourself if you have "crossed over" from an employee mindset to a business-owner mindset. This is a passage that you must make if you are to survive—and thrive—in the shoals of entrepreneurning. Then you must learn the ins and outs of financial planning, sales, marketing and managing people—all of which Ron Guzik writes about from long-time hands-on experience.

If you use this book well, you will walk through all of the planning steps you need to avoid disaster and enhance your chances of building a venture that you will be proud of and that will earn a good living for you and your family.

— Marc Kramer

President, Kramer Communications
Author of *Financing & Building an
E-Commerce Venture* (Prentice Hall, 2001)
Small Business Turnaround (Adams Media, 1999)
Power Networking (NTC Publishing, 1997)

Work is love made visible.
— Khalil Gibran

INTRODUCTION

Whether you are an established business or a recent start-up, I hope you will find the information contained in this book accessible and easy to apply to your business immediately to help you reach your goals. That should allow you and your people to prosper and enjoy your work.

I have organized the book into twenty-nine short, condensed chapters. Each chapter is a self-contained piece and stands as a complete set of ideas and tools for that topic. Chapters are designed to be a quick read for the busy entrepreneur all the while conveying powerful and useful concepts and techniques. This will save you from wasting time and energy making mistakes or searching high and low for needed information. Most chapters include additional resources to assist you in further growth and development.

The book can be read cover to cover for a full course on business development—a mini-MBA class for entrepreneurs, if you will. Or you can go directly to the section where you want to concentrate your attention, say Sales or Marketing, and read several chapters in that area. This gives you a broad yet incisive view of a function or area including complementary concepts and techniques to deepen your understanding and sharpen your skills.

Finally, you can select a particular individual topic of concern (making your loan proposal better, for example) and focus right away on your most pressing concern.

Whichever approach you choose, I trust you will find the book filled with material to be read, and re-read, whenever you are faced with a business problem, need to make a change or map out a strategy.

The book is organized into eight sections to make it easy to go directly to the section that you want to focus your attention on or that you are struggling with. Each section contains from two to five chapters on the subject. The eight sections are:

- *You, the entrepreneur*
- *Planning*
- *Making your plan happen*
- *Business development*
- *Finance*
- *Sales*
- *Marketing*
- *Management*

These eight sections cover the A to Z of business growth and development. May your reading and reflection on these topics help you Build Your Business Stronger--And Do It Quickly!

Good luck, and Godspeed on your journey.

Carol Stream, Illinois
November 2001

ACKNOWLEDGMENTS

Many people have helped make this book possible, either by their direct involvement in the concept or in the writing, or by their unflagging support. First of all, my family—Bev and Jim Guzik, Jim, Elisa, Ashley and Alexandra Guzik, Linda, Bruce, Christopher and Nicole Watson, and Patti Olson—have been major pillars of support. I love you and appreciate all of your encouragement. My life is also richer because of a number of special friends: Sheila Lange, Chris Duros, Nancy and Richard Hartmann, Jamie and Leslie Henderson, Kathy Hirsch, Kathy Corra, Tim and Karen Sheehan, Jim and Carlene Gruber, Laura Aanenson, Peg Miller, Kathryn Furtek, Susan Francis, Mary Elizabeth Murphy, Roger Coon, Elida Hinojosa, Jeff Johnson, Zanne Gray, Bruce Anderson, Sandy Karn and Anil Saxena. Thank you for being so good for me.

Jill Cleary-Svoboda and Al Svoboda from *Svoboda's Business Magazine*, where the material in most of these chapters was first published, have been immensely supportive and a joy to work with. Thank you to everyone at the Village of Bellwood; you have treated me so well as we collaborated at work. A special thanks goes to Janet Tallberg who helped me with my early writings. Your help was—and is—greatly appreciated. I similarly value the support I've received from Lawrence Watson, the Tuesday and Saturday groups, and Fox Valley Unity.

More than any other individual, Patrick Grace deserves enormous thanks for the making of this book. I very much appreciate his hard work, support, encouragement, caring and friendship. As a collaborating writer and editor, he not only made the book happen but made it a much better book. I couldn't have done this book without him and my life is richer because he is in it. The staff at Grace Associates/editorial consultants has been great. Shannon Luther performs miracles keeping things organized. Amanda Ballard does amazing work in marketing. Mark Phillips from Marketing+Design Group executed the stunning cover and page layouts. Jennifer Adkins did a great job with the copy editing. I want to thank Shannon Luther and Jason Thacker for modelling for the cover. Jan Dickinson did some wonderful drawings that really enhanced the book. Sharon Johnson, once again, did a superb index.

Many other people shared ideas, made suggestions or reviewed the material for the book including Laura Aanenson, Jamie Henderson, Mary Elizabeth Murphy, Peg Miller, and Sharon Haley.

To all of the above, my heartfelt thanks—and hopes for blessings in your work and in the other parts of your life as well.

DEDICATION

To entrepreneurs everywhere—
Your courage, perseverence, vision and
creative energy are a constant inspiration to me
and to all who aspire to own and manage
their own business.

YOU, THE ENTREPRENEUR

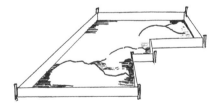

BUILD

CHAPTER 1

From Employee to Entrepreneur

Crossing Over to a Business Mindset

There is nothing either good or bad, but thinking makes it so.

— William Shakespeare, **Hamlet II:2**

A friend who's been a solo consultant for eighteen months tells me that he feels like he's in the middle of one of those perilous rope bridges swinging over a gorge in the Himalayas. "I've left the security of a salary, and I'm trying to cross over to being a successful entrepreneur, but I'm only halfway there," he remarked recently. "To crawl back to being salaried or else go forward and make it to a secure niche as a business person both seem terribly hard."

This individual is learning a highly important lesson: to survive as an entrepreneur, you have to learn new ways of thinking and acting. Old habits that supported you in the corporate or public sector now may hurt you, like a shoe sole worn through. Survival techniques that worked on the salaried side of that Himalayan gorge can be a prescription for disaster if you count on them in your solo venture.

A New Vision of Your World

In a quite concrete way, you need to see things around you differently. People whom you once identified only as neighbors or as passersby in your town square may now be potential customers. Banks you drive past that you used to ignore may now bear exploring as sources of capital. Advertisements that you barely glanced at may now be a springboard for creative marketing ideas, so they should be studied carefully.

Here's a metaphor that may help:

Have you ever radically changed the model of car you drive, say from a sedate sedan to a dazzling sports car? Before you took the plunge, you were unaware of the number of sports models on the road with you. Within a week or two after buying your own, however, you notice a huge number of similar models all around you. Has the market suddenly become flooded with sports cars? No. The change is in you. You just changed the filter through which you look out upon the world.

Ideally, your switch to self-employment ought to outfit you with just such a new filter and give you the capacity to enjoy a new vision of the world.

As you shift from relying upon a regular job to being in business for yourself, you necessarily undertake to trade in a number of "mental models" for different ones. A mental model or mindset is a fairly entrenched belief about how we should conduct ourselves as we interface with the world around us. We harbor mindsets relating to every aspect of life, everything from money (how to earn it, save it, spend it) to family or social relations, and, of course, to business. We "know" that life just is a certain way in each of these areas, and we carry these certitudes around in our heads.

Such mental models are shaped early in life. They help us categorize and cope with an astonishing variety of circumstances in our lives. That's the good part. The problem comes when we are unconscious of or overly attached to certain mental models and can't relinquish or modify them so we can adapt our thoughts and actions to new circumstances.

So these old rock-solid verities need to be challenged. Let's look at some cases in point.

On the job, you felt secure running up the limit on your credit cards because there'd always be next month's paycheck to help you pay it off. When you're on your own, undisciplined personal debt can wipe you out.

Your salaried self earned money and thus felt liberated to spend it. The entrepreneurial mode, however, dictates belt tightening on personal expenses but a willingness to spend—even risk—money on nurturing your fledgling enterprise.

For example, one woman who had valuable analytical skills she wanted to sell to major corporations on a consultancy basis tried to do her brochures "on the cheap." Lacking resources, she hand-lettered the copy and did her own photocopying and folding. She struck out at every single corporation she included in her mailing, most likely because her brochure looked unprofessional. She should have earned or borrowed the $500 or so it would have cost to do the brochures right.

Another example: Employees are trained to specialize. Usually, in large corporations, the more specialized a person is, the better. As an entrepreneur—unless you have the means to hire a staff at the outset—you have to be not only a crackerjack at providing a service or turning out a product, you are also going to have to be chief cook, bottle washer, and handholder of all and sundry. In other words, you have to be a great generalist.

Employees are typically brought into a work environment that is already very structured. Veterans help them fit into a pre-existing pattern and show them the right way to perform the tasks in their job description. In corporate America, much is locked in.

In sharp contrast, the entrepreneur starts with absolutely no structures in place. As the creator of your venture, you will have to devise your own structures from Day One (and often you'll make mistakes and be forced to re-do those structures).

Business owners also need self-discipline. While this is also a laudable trait in a corporate setting, few corporations rely on it. Big companies build in checkpoints and supervision to insure that even those who lack such discipline will fit the mold. When you're marketing your own venture, you are the only one who's going to make something happen. If you don't do it, you will have to close up shop and go back to studying help-wanted ads.

Stay in a Marketing Mode

One of the hardest things you'll have to swallow in your role as an entrepreneur is the constant need to market yourself and your product or service. Attendees at networking breakfasts have repeatedly heard the stories of entrepreneurs who seemed to have it made, churning out work for a few clients and downplaying the need to continually market what they could provide. Then a major client switches to another provider, a second goes bankrupt, and a third one starts slacking off on orders. Zap! The entrepreneur is left with close to zero billables while all his accounts payable remain due.

What should you do if you recognize that you have remained stuck in a salaried employee mindset while you are struggling to develop your own business? First, you must develop an awareness of your models and the need to adjust them, and then you must force yourself into action. A good place to start is by developing friendships with successful business owners in your own sector or, really, in almost any sector. This might mean joining the chamber of commerce or Kiwanis Club or else simply signing up with a local networking group.

Other possibilities include professional or trade associations. Whether you're an accountant, a secretary, a sales representative or a restaurateur, there's probably a group of your peers already formed and meeting regularly. If not, consider starting one. Since we absorb and acquire the mental models of people around us, this action will make a difference.

Reading articles and books written by fellow entrepreneurs or researchers who have made entrepreneurship their passionate focus is another wonderful way to steer your mental models into more productive directions.

Two I recommend highly are

* *The Fifth Discipline: The Art and Practice of the Learning Organization*, by Peter Senge (Doubleday, 1990)
* *Making it on Your Own: Surviving and Thriving on the Ups and Downs of Being Your own Boss*, by Paul and Sarah Edwards (Putnam, 1991).

A man's mind stretched by a new idea can never go back to its original dimensions.

— Oliver Wendell Holmes, Jr.

We are shifting from a managerial society to an entrepreneurial society.

— John Naisbitt, author, **Megatrends**

He who knows much about others may be learned, but he who understands himself is more intelligent. He who controls others may be powerful, but he who has mastered himself is mightier still.

— Lao-Tsu

No great improvements in the lot of mankind are possible until a great change takes place in the fundamental constitution of their modes of thought.

— John Stuart Mill

Being in your own business is working 80 hours a week so that you can avoid working 40 hours a week for someone else.

— Ramona E. F. Arnett, President,
   Ramona Enterprises

Trust yourself. You know more than you think you do.

— Benjamin Spock, M.D.

What we must decide is how we are valuable rather than how valuable we are.

— Edgar J. Friedenberg

CHAPTER 2

Getting Your Priorities Straight

Entrepreneurial Values— Why You Should Know What Yours Are

I would rather be well versed about myself than about Cicero;
in the experience I have about myself I find enough
to make me wise.

— Michel de Montaigne

The values you hold and the way in which you rank those values (highest, second highest and so) on are absolutely critical for your chances of successfully launching and developing a business. It follows that a basic exercise for entrepreneurs is to take to heart and to work through that famous tenet of Socrates: "Know thyself."

As a consultant and adult-education teacher in entrepreneurship, I have seen this borne out time and again in my clients' and students' ventures. As a result, I have come to emphasize it strongly in my workshops.

Examples of values, in the sense in which Anthony Robbins (author of *Unlimited Power* and *Awaken the Giant Within*) uses the term, would be such abstractions as "challenge," "fun," "freedom," "control," "self-expression," "integrity," "power," "love," "success," and "family."

Every entrepreneur will differ in his or her range of values, and in the way he or she sets priorities on them.

Some such values, however, are, in my experience, absolutely fundamental for success in new businesses. I would say, in fact, that "integrity," "ethics," "excellence," and "hard work" will always be close to the top of the hierarchy for successful entrepreneurs.

The Entrepreneurial Top Ten

To fill out the rest of the "Top Ten" in entrepreneurial values is not as easy, and there is plenty of room for debate among startup specialists. My personal list would include "service to customers and to society," "recognition or acknowledgment" (by others), "sense of making a difference," "family," "success," and "personal growth." "Money," as such, is not a value, just a barometer that measures other values, such as "success."

Another point: Some people may be surprised that I name "family" as an entrepreneurial value. Stereotypes held in the public mind often cast entrepreneurs as swashbuckling adventurers and/or workaholics ready to sacrifice family life for monetary success—and also daredevils who fear no evil, not even bankruptcy. Obviously, a certain percentage of startups do have such types at the helm. But the vast majority of entrepreneurs whom I've followed are quite concerned about their families and about keeping things in balance.

"Security" is an interesting subject. Contrary to popular opinion, most entrepreneurs are not big risk takers. Rather, they are people who have studied the risks of a certain undertaking and have made a calculated decision that the risks are worth taking and that they have a decent chance of success. In short, while they are used to taking a certain amount of risk, they are not simply people who would roll double or nothing.

Entrepreneurs can better be described as "managers of risks." They are always asking themselves, "What's the risk here? Is it manageable? If so, how can I manage it?"

Your values are, typically, developed from age three to ten or twelve through repetition in the family, at school, and among friends. A certain amount of change is possible, but going against the grain of your childhood can be extremely painful. So it really does matter if you can identify and rank your values.

Discover Your Values

Robbins suggests that we simply ask ourselves, "What is more important to me—love or security or fun (or whatever)?" If the answer is "love," you can go on to another set of possibilities: "OK, then, is 'love' more important than 'honesty' or 'fidelity' or 'reputation' and so on?" Finally, you'll get a one-through-ten list. After some second-guessing and rearranging of your list, you will have established your hierarchy of values.

Your list can then serve as a guideline for whether you should really start or continue in this or that venture or perhaps go back to the drawing board. If, for example, one of your highest values is "fun," you might do well opening a skiing school but not so well as the owner of a Laundromat. If you put "family" near the top, you may not want to own that restaurant—unless your spouse and kids are wild about hard work and long hours too.

Not only should your values be congruent with those of your spouse (unless having a satisfying marriage is not important to you), they should also mesh with the values of the people you hire. If you place a high priority on ethics, don't saddle yourself with fast-and-loose types. If you like structure, bring on people who can live with structure.

If you value courtesy and friendliness, forget the sourpusses. And so on.

You will find, among other things, that if your employees share your basic values, you'll be much more able to motivate them than if you are struggling with a conflict of values. If all they want to do is have fun and you are really into hard work, you can count on problems. But if, on the other hand, both you and they like to lock up at five or six on the dot and get home to family, you share a basic understanding about life—and on this score, at least, you'll get along fine.

Much of the unhappiness we encounter in life results from our getting into conflict with our values. I was once part of a partnership with a man who had spent his entire working life in large, very structured companies; his tolerance for uncertainty was low, which is to say he placed a very high value on security. The pressure of independence became too much for him, and we had to break up the venture.

Interestingly enough, such things can change. I ran into him recently, and he was on the verge of leaving a corporate job and getting out on his own in business. Obviously, security has moved down a few notches on his hierarchy of values and, clearly, independence has moved up.

BUSINESS PLANNING

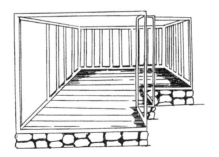

BUILD YOUR

Goals—Yardstick for Productivity

Setting Goals for Your Business

People are not lazy. They simply have impotent goals—that is, goals that do not inspire them.

— Anthony Robbins

Without goals, you will have nothing to measure productivity against. Goals are an absolute "given" in any effort to maximize personal productivity. What is more, someone wiser than I has remarked, "Goals aren't goals until you write them down." What you just keep in your head has a way of becoming nebulous, and less than compelling as a motivating force. So please. . . write your goals down!

There are three levels of goals to which you should pay attention. All are important, and each level interlocks with the others, but the levels are distinct.

1. Long-term goals. Project these out at least five years. Say where you would like to be then and what you want your venture to look like. For instance, we will be a $2 million company in annual sales, with at least ten employees and an attractive headquarters of at least 2,000 square feet. Do not, however, limit long-term goals to the

purely financial. You might say, as well, we will be a close-knit team and have in place effective systems for taking in suggestions, resolving differences, deciding on priorities and courses of action, and each person will have an opportunity for rejuvenating vacation time and profit sharing as we grow.

2. Medium-term goals. These are for the period from the year in progress to, say, four years down the road. This level might include an ideal percentage of growth—whatever you think is reasonable and manageable—8 percent, 12 percent, 25 percent or more. Such goals might also include a plan for customer development—adding ten new clients a year, for example, for an advertising agency or a market-research firm, achieving 80 percent occupancy for a motel, or a certain volume of diners for breakfast, lunch, and dinner for a restaurant. This level could also take in additions to, or upgrading of, your essential equipment, tools, and vehicle for a landscaping service, PC stations and sophistication of software for an office operation, etc. Spell these things out in careful detail. How can you expect to get what you need unless you determine just what it is, and write it down?

3. Short-term goals. Depending on your enterprise, these could be virtually day by day, or week by week, or possibly goals on a monthly or quarterly basis. (In some instances, you might need to set goals for all these different periods of time.)

Start on Your Goals

You will need more space than I'm providing you here to do an adequate job of writing down your goals. However, I'm going to get you started. After all, there's no time like the present. Take a moment and begin to sketch goals for each of the three levels. Promise yourself, though, that you will carry forth this assignment into either a notebook or a poster or a file folder labeled "goals." Make a commitment, too, to keep revising your goals as you develop your business; some you set now may turn out to be too ambitious or unrealistic; others may actually turn out to be too limiting or wimpy.

My long-term goals for my business are:
1..
2..
3..

My medium-term goals for my business are:
1..
2..
3..
4..
5..

My short-term goals for my business are:
1..
2..
3..
4..
5..
6..
7..
8..
9..
10..
11..
12..

The act of writing down goals is a declaration of your

commitment to them. It is as if you are telling the universe, "Hey, I'm serious about this!" As W.H. Murray said in *The Scottish Himalayan Expedition*, "Until one is committed, there is hesitancy, the chance to draw back, always ineffectiveness. Concerning all acts of initiative (and creation) there is one elementary truth, the ignorance of which kills countless plans: that the moment one definitely commits oneself, then Providence moves, too."

Include Target Dates

Look back over your goals now. Have you included a target date for each level? The setting of a date (which can in some cases be approximate) for achievement of this or that goal is key to productivity. A target date, you will find, also supports keeping you focused, on track, and in action.

There is definitely a place for setting goals for intangibles, such as achieving a certain level of harmony among your staff, or "flow," or heightened awareness, etc. These are worthwhile endeavors, but are, unfortunately, much harder to track. Try therefore to link these goals to specific behaviors or actions; in other words, keep them as concrete and practical as possible. Just to take one example, a goal for improved harmony among staff might be translated into something like having everybody keep an informal scoresheet of misunderstandings, snubbing type behavior, failure to keep everybody in the loop informed, etc. You don't want names, nor specifics, just numbers of incidents such as these per month. When you see the scoresheet totals of everybody on your staff going down progressively, you'll know you are making progress toward harmony.

CHAPTER 4

Want to See Success?

Get the Big Picture First

One doesn't discover new lands without consenting to lose sight of the shore for a very long time.

— André Gide

To achieve success, you must first envision it.

Put another way, if you don't know where you are going, you're very likely to end up someplace you don't want to be.

This is the first hard lesson of strategic planning. Those who plod along day by day in businesses that are stuck "in the way we've always done it," businesses whose growth is lackluster or practically nil, usually are suffering from a lack of creative strategic planning. And that kind of planning always involves vision—looking one, three, five years down the road and actually picturing the way your operation will look.

"Start with the end in mind," Stephen Covey, author of *The Seven Habits of Highly Effective People*, counsels his devotees. Then plan backward from there.

Should your gallery of humorous art be franchised? Should you plan to sell your market research operation conglomerate? Will you need a business partner with financial resources to fuel the expansion of your graphic arts firm? These may not be the things you want to consider for the year in progress. But how about two or three years from now?

Marianne is a financial planner who wants to build up her accounts. She has tried any number of business development techniques, such as networking and expanding the services she offers, but she has come to realize that she needs an integrated plan. To help her write one, she has contracted for some time with a small-business coach.

Where Are You Today?

Here are the guidelines her coach lays down for Marianne:

1. Put down, on paper, where you and your business are today. What are your financials? Who are your customers? What's the competition like? How about your working space and your equipment? Products and services?

Marianne writes down: Last year's gross $87,000; last year's net, $61,000; income resulting from 36 clients on a fee basis (sliding scale according to the amounts invested). Competition: Six other independent financial planners in the area, plus those working for banks, insurance companies and brokerage firms. Still working from home office, with old 486 PC and rudimentary printer and copier. Paying off $5,000 credit card loan ($265/month) and car loan ($220/month).

2. Where would like to see yourself and your business in one year?

Marianne writes: Twenty percent increase in gross

revenues and 22 percent increase in net revenues, downtown office in Class A space, modest upgrades in office equipment, and reorganization of personal debts to total, after mortgage payment, no more than $350/month.

3. Where would like to see yourself in three years?

This time she puts down: Working on 10 to 15 percent annual growth, maintain downtown space, be incorporated, have a full-time personal assistant, all new office furniture and late-model office equipment, have an upscale automobile owned by the business and have enough money to take four weeks' vacation and go someplace far away.

Marianne has now traveled far down the road toward developing an effective strategic plan for future growth. There are, however, two more components she needs to add:

1. An analysis of her strengths and weaknesses.
2. An action plan for achieving her goals.

Identify Your Strengths and Weaknesses

Strengths and weaknesses should be divided into external and internal categories. The external category is usually called "Opportunities and Threats." Under "Opportunities," Marianne list such things as opportunities in the community to expand her client base—that is, numbers of people who have some awareness of the benefits of financial planning but who have not yet sought help from a professional. Under "Threats," she lists competition, state and local restrictions, and the general image of financial planners in the public mind. (For example, does the public believe them to be trustworthy? Knowledgeable? Concerned for their clients' well-being?)

In the internal category, Marianne needs to look at herself personally—her own beliefs or mindsets about such things as personal selling, organization (including time management), pricing her services, interactions with existing clients, and so on.

Marianne goes through her list of questions and decides that there is indeed an opportunity with increased awareness in her community of the importance of financial planning, as well as with a growing population of aging seniors ready to listen to a professional. She also finds that most of her competition has not yet personalized their services; each seems to represent some large institution of the kind much of the public perceives as being impersonal.

Among her internal strengths Marianne counts her knowledge of finance, her people skills, and her knack for organization. Her weaknesses, she finds, include her lack of discipline in pursuing new business and her tendency to be satisfied with outdated business equipment.

With the surfacing of both the external and internal data, Marianne is now ready to tackle the drafting of an action plan.

Here is what she decides:

1. She will increase the time she spends with her coach and be more diligent about carrying out the coach's suggestions for growing the business.

2. She will attend a top-drawer seminar for consulting professionals on cultivating clients and expanding a client base.

3. She will actively seek referrals from existing clients in order to broaden her client base.

4. She will be disciplined about following up on referrals, keeping her appointments, and writing thank-you notes to those who have provided referrals.

5. She will contract with a local temporary-help agency

to hire an assistant one or two days a week to handle routine clerical chores and free up more time for marketing and research of financial services. (This, Marianne decides, will be a good step toward one of her goals: Hiring a full-time personal assistant.)

Shape a Strategy for Your Business

A strategy for business development often takes the form of one, or a combination, of four generic strategies. These four are

1. Price
2. Quality
3. Service
4. Location

What you want to aim for is having the best of one or a combination of these four factors. And you should choose what you focus on to match up to both external and internal strengths. For instance, Marianne might choose service because she believes that her own personal warmth and caringness (an internal strength) will out-duel the impersonality of the large institutions that offer financial planning. She might also choose to focus on the senior citizen population because they offer larger numbers of prospective clients than any other age group (an external strength/opportunity).

You should not try to be all things to all people. It is virtually impossible to be superior in all four factors, and you might go crazy trying. Some who have tried have ended up being mediocre in all four areas and not standing out in any one way.

I'd like to mention a book that I've found to be very helpful. It's called *Competitive Strategy: Techniques for Analyzing Industries and Competitors*, by Michael Porter,

Ph.D. (1980). The first edition of this book was published over twenty years ago, and it's now considered the standard work in the area of strategy. It's not easy reading—it requires close attention and concentration—but you don't have to read it cover to cover. The first and second chapters alone provide an amazing amount of very powerful material. You should be able to find a copy at your local library or bookstore.

———————

The chief characteristic of the volitional act is the existence of a purpose to be achieved; the clear vision of an aim.

   — Roberto Assagioli, ***The Act of Will***

In the long run men hit only what they aim at.

   — Henry David Thoreau

If you want a place in the sun, you must leave the shade of the family tree.

   — Osage Saying

CHAPTER 5

Plan to Capitalize on Your Strengths and Shore Up Your Weaknesses

Make Your Planning Painless— And Take Your Business to the Top

The best way to predict the future is to create it.

— Peter Drucker

Let's dust off a long-forgotten chestnut in business-speak—"Plan your work, then work your plan"—and make it our centerpiece. Planning is often the most talked-about and least acted-upon component in the business process. And lack of adequate or well-reasoned planning is among the more fatal maladies that beset new or even established enterprises. It doesn't have to be that way.

With a surprisingly modest investment of time and energy each week, you can get results like this:

- Better day-to-day focus.
- Appropriate ranking of your business, so that the biggest need receives the biggest chunk of your creativity and energy and so on down the line.
- Better managerial and staff preparation—to handle the unexpected.
- More effective decision making.
- Greatly reduced stress.

Sound convincing? Then let's get into it!

At the most fundamental level, good business planning asks and answers three straightforward questions:

1) Where are you right now?

2) Where do you need to go?

3) How will you get there?

Flying an airplane or steering a sailboat provides us with an analogy. You've got to get that craft off the ground or away from the safety of a mooring or anchor, move across a patch of sky or sea with unpredictable weather conditions and the possibility of unexpected challenges, and land securely in another location. Not easy, but doable if you have a good knowledge of your equipment, your teammates, your route, and you are very clear in your mind about what your destination is. As Yogi Berra once said, "If you don't know where you're going, you'll probably end up someplace else."

What Does Success Look Like?

Let's borrow some questions from Michael E. Gerber's bestseller, *The E-Myth Revisited*, because as Gerber aptly points out, if you don't know what your success will look or feel like, you can't expect to achieve it. So, with Gerber, let's ask ourselves:

• What do I wish my business (or my life) to look like?

• How do I ideally want to run my business on a day-by-day basis?

• What kind of relations do I want to have with my partners, employees, suppliers, customers?

• How do I want people to think about me?

• How much money will I need to accomplish the things I wish to do? By when will I need it?

All the microplanning in the world—fighting the little

skirmishes that crop up in business or trying to plug the hole in the dike when an ocean of problems threatens to overwhelm you—won't give you anything more than a mish-mash unless you get the macro picture clear in your head.

Do you see yourself as the head of a firm of 3, 15, 50 or 200 people? Are you really going to be happy keeping your entire operation in the anteroom off the kitchen? Are you a solo entrepreneur? Or someone best suited for a partnership? Do you want to grow yourself into being bought out by a large company that will provide you with a solid contract and ample autonomy? Just what is it you really want? An astonishing number of entrepreneurs never get around to asking—or answering—these questions, to the detriment of their own growth and that of their firm.

Resolve now that you aren't going to be one of them!

Cut to the Nitty-Gritty

Only after you have dealt with the "big picture" questions and answers should you turn to the nitty-gritty questions. Then you need to relate all questions on this micro-level to the macro-level conception of just how you'd like your business and your life to develop.

On that micro-level, however, here are some of the key questions you must ask yourself:
- Where am I right now in my business development?
- What has gone on in and around my business over the last year? (Both the positive and the negatives, please!)
- What are the problems and opportunities I am facing at this moment?
- What is the next level of development to which I'd like to take my venture?

Let's replay both the macro and the micro levels of planning with a fictional fellow we'll call John Rosen, who is going into his second year of owning and managing a hardware store in a bustling suburban location.

On the macro level John would like to "get above it all," and have plenty of free time for his family, leisure pursuits and charitable endeavors. This means taking the store to a level where it produces a good income for him and for the full-time manager he hopes to hire in two or three years.

John's goals in life include much more than successfully running a hardware store. He'd like to get involved in socially conscientious civic and church drives and be a positive force in his suburban community. He also hopes to send his three children to academically challenging colleges and see them happily launched into rewarding careers. And he and his wife Nancy would like to take one major trip a year and get to know other countries.

So John is fulfilling the prime requirement for being able to deal with the nitty-gritty day-by-day questions of managing a business: He is very clear about the picture into which he wants to fit himself and his family on the macro level.

Factors You Can Control

Now, on the micro-level, the nuts and bolts: John begins by writing down that he is still working out the kinks in inventory control, development of sales clerks, and advertising. He feels his first year has been too hit or miss. Sales were enough to keep the store in the black, but just barely. John wonders how he can get better control of his overhead, sharpen his advertising appeal and targeting, and get his new clerks to be more sales-oriented without being pushy.

These are all internal questions—things that depend directly upon him and his employees.

Factors You Can't Control

After he has framed these items on paper, John turns to the external questions—those that depend upon factors mostly outside his control. Such items may be considered either opportunities or threats, according to John's perceptions of them, and would include factors such as tax rates, government regulations (existing or pending), changes in product lines he stocks, market trends, competition, disposable income among his clientele, and customer expectations.

John's analysis of his internal realities breaks down into lists of strengths and weaknesses.

On the "strengths" side John puts his own strong motivation and his growing knowledge of the industry, along with the good will of his employees. He counts as "weaknesses" his so-so grip on inventory control, the shakiness of his advertising program thus far, and his employees' lack of comfort with trying to generate sales.

Then John moves on to the external side and does a similar breakdown of pluses and minuses. Here he decides his biggest strength is the booming interest in home renovation, especially of the do-it-yourself variety. However, others have also taken note of the market, for John's greatest external threat appears to stem from the large building supplies store that has just opened in a shopping center a mile away.

Taking Action

While the rock-bottom for good planning is taking stock of existing realities, both internal and external, this is just a first step. Nothing will change unless John develops action plans for capitalizing on his strengths and shoring up his weaknesses.

This is the tough part. Putting yourself into John's shoes, you may quickly come to realize that several heads are better than one, and this indeed is what John himself decides. He sets up a program of consultations to rummage through his options. John schedules planning sessions with his banker, his accountant, a good personal friend in another line of business, his marketing consultant, his spouse, and also his employees.

After their rounds of consultations, plus several brainstorming sessions in which he brings together people from diverse backgrounds, John sketches in his plan. Over the next six months, he decides, he will

• Send himself to a seminar on inventory control and also look around for a consultant in this area who can backstop his decisions.

• Buy videotapes on retail salesmanship for his employees to watch together and provide a festive atmosphere for them to do this in—soft drinks and snacks.

• Budget 10 percent more for advertising than the previous year and aim to develop more special promotions to increase traffic.

• With big marketing consultant, devise a program to build customer loyalty to his store in the face of the competition from the large chain store down the road.

A final caveat. Be careful not to take your strengths for granted and give them little attention while you are trying to bolster your weak spots. The whole array of strengths and weaknesses deserves your attention as you plan, enact new programs, and monitor how it is all working out.

Section III

MAKING YOUR PLAN HAPPEN

BUILD YOUR BUSINESS

The Art of Implementing Your Strategic Plan

You must do the thing that you think you cannot do.

— Eleanor Roosevelt

You have made your vision of success concrete by building a strategic action plan for your business. Now, to carry out that vision, you as a business owner need a deep and practical appreciation of two qualities that can be as hard to pin down as they are important. You might not even think of them right off the bat—they are emotional intelligence (EI) and synergy.

"Whoa!" some of you might say. "I'm not even sure what you're talking about, much less how it could help my business—or how I can learn how to do it."

Until Daniel Goleman published his book *Emotional Intelligence*, the notion of analyzing and trying to make the best use of feelings was seldom advanced. It was not exactly the kind of thing you would discuss at a chamber of commerce meeting or a small business seminar. Thanks to Goleman, however, now it's a hot item.

Why is that? It's because Goleman has shown us how

the emotional components of our personality, or our "style," affect how we present ourselves and our products. These same emotional aspects, we have learned, also affect the degree of productivity we achieve in our relations with our partners, employees, suppliers, and customers.

EI, Not IQ, Can Carry the Day

Your skill in identifying, experiencing, and expressing emotions is key to building good rapport with the people who make up your work life. And relationships are at the heart of what makes a business succeed.

A critical difference between strategic planning—which will give you a road map of where you want to take your business—and executing your plan is that while you may be able to plan by yourself, implementing the plan almost always requires the participation of other people. Being able to read people and understand their psychological and emotional make-up will take you far toward relating with each of them "where they live."

A salesman, for example, who can sense that a prospective customer is having a tough day (behind on invoicing or facing employee relations problems or some other such difficulty) will be able to say something like, "Gee, I'm sorry. You seem to be having a rough day. Instead of my showing you these samples now, could I make an appointment to stop by and see you next week?"

The owner-manager of an office or plant operation who is sensitive to people's moods or physical conditions may be able to notice that someone on the staff is ill and really ought to go home—even if that person herself may want to tough it out or not be a bother. An employee invited to take the afternoon off and get some rest will not soon forget the perceptiveness and good will of a supervisor.

These are examples of productive emotional intelligence operating in the workplace. Goleman, in fact, says that emotional intelligence is even more important than the standard IQ (or intelligence quotient) in determining whether a person will be a success at work. In other words, emotional savvy counts more than being brainy or clever.

Carrying out an action plan inevitably involves delegating aspects of the plan to others, not only employees but also people offering business-to-business services. These people might include a market research firm, a freelance graphic artist, an accountant, or a copy center, for instance. How you present yourself and how you negotiate and collaborate with these providers to achieve your desired results will make all the difference in whether your projects succeed or fail.

Emotional intelligence can be developed through personal awareness workshops; through coaching and counseling; through feedback from family, friends and associates, as well as through reading, reflecting, and even meditating. But it definitely requires a commitment. The trick is to get to know yourself very, very well and then make incremental adjustments in your behavior, especially in the area of fine tuning your communication style.

The Role of Synergy

Synergy is the second quality needed for turning a plan into a series of well-executed steps that bring you the results you have envisioned. All operations have synergy—or the phenomenon of different talents and techniques combining to produce a result that is beyond what any single talent or technique would have achieved alone. Brainstorming with a group is a good example of synergy in action.

The decisions you make as you implement your strategic plan should be strongly supported by the research and planning you did during the strategizing stage. The more information you gathered and processed, and the better you and your team understand the challenges facing your business, the better equipped you will be to effectively carry out the day-by-day activities you built into your plan.

This, then, is the synergistic combining of strategic planning with execution.

Whether it is in developing and executing an advertising campaign, in setting up and operating an inventory control system, or putting together an effective customer relations policy, synergy will always play a role. And the more you can step back and appreciate the contributions of various individuals working with you—with their different talents, personalities, and energy levels—the better able you will be to bolster and guide the synergistic effects that will spell success.

The criticial ingredient is getting off your butt and doing something. It's as simple as that. A lot of people have ideas, but there are few who decide to do something about them now. Not tomorrow. Not next week. But today. The true entrepreneur is a doer, not a dreamer.

— Nolan Bushnell, founder, Atari

Life is either a daring adventure or nothing.

— Helen Keller

Turn Goals into Reality

Create an Action Plan

Let me tell you the secret that has led me to my goal.
My strength lies solely in my tenacity.

— Louis Pasteur

Imagine yourself embarking on a trek through a rugged and unfamiliar mountainous region. You wouldn't hesitate to locate and hire the best guide you could find, would you? After all, with a capable guide, you could plot out a detailed course and plan of attack. This would greatly reduce your risks by showing you just where you'd be on the trail and giving you estimated times of arrivals for various benchmarks.

Isn't the plunge into carving out a healthy market share in whatever field you're in comparable to a trek through challenging and unfamiliar terrain? Don't you therefore owe it to yourself to secure and follow a good guide?

The guide you need is an action plan.

Use this chapter as a guide for developing your own action plan. Please don't stop with just this chapter, however. Take advantage of all the resources you can muster, especially a local Service Corps of Retired Executives

(SCORE) chapter, trusted friends with business savvy, your banker, your accountant, community college small business development centers, seminars, and short courses.

What makes up an action plan?

Focus on Specific Actions

First, focus on specific actions, the more specific the better. Not only should you write them down, point by point, you should call and tell at least one other person who has a personal or professional interest in your success (spouse, banker, key employee, and so on.) It helps to have someone else on your side.

On our hypothetical mountain trip, specific examples of actions might include hiking along a charted trail for four miles, eating lunch and relaxing for an hour or so, hiking another three or four miles, and then setting up camp for the night.

Likewise, a plan for expanding your business might include developing a promotional piece, mailing it, calling all the businesses that respond, setting up appointments, and delivering sales presentations. The more clearly defined each step is, the more likely you are to actually accomplish it.

Set Target Dates

Second, set a target date for each step. Do I hear moans and groans out there? Few of us like deadlines, whether we set them ourselves or someone else sets them for us. Deadlines seem to transform us from creators to victims. Circled dates on the calendar above our desks look like eagles ready to pounce and devour us.

Here we need to shift our perception from seeing the

achievement of target dates as "good" or "bad" to seeing them simply as helpful guideposts. Too often we think, in moralizing fashion, that not finishing a project by a deadline, or not coming in under budget, is just plain "bad." True, we should do all in our power to meet deadlines and budgeted projections, but we should also be ready to cut ourselves some slack if the unexpected or the unavoidable causes delays or added expense.

Let's reconsider our mountain trek. Just because you failed to reach the ideal campsite by nightfall doesn't make the whole trip a disaster. What would really be negative would be giving up the goal of reaching the mountain top entirely, rather than being willing to adjust the number of hours—or even days—it will take you to get there.

Have a Fallback Strategy

A good action plan in business always allows flexibility for a fallback strategy. Call it "Plan B" or "regrouping" or whatever you like, but do stand ready to give yourself second chances to reach both interim and ultimate goals.

Finally, be sure each step is small enough to be identifiably separate from other steps because:

It's easier to organize a series of small steps, and you are more likely to get started and keep yourself moving through the steps if each step seems as if it can be managed with a reasonable outlay of effort. Remember the relevant law from Newtonian physics: A body at rest will tend to remain at rest; a body in motion will tend to remain in motion.

The ideal size for a step in a business project is highly individual. Some people prefer to have real baby steps, while others motivate themselves by making each step fairly ambitious.

Make Giant Steps into Small Ones

If, however, you find yourself balking at carrying out your action plan, one problem may be that you have created steps that are larger than your energy level can handle. If you suspect that's the case, break down your overly large steps into smaller, achievable ones. For example, "developing a promotional piece" can be broken down into smaller steps like this:

1. Brainstorm with staff and friends,
2. Take the best ideas to a marketing consultant for refining,
3. Rough out the piece,
4. Refine the piece,
5. Get printing bids,
6. Choose a printer, and
7. Produce piece in X quantity.

What you want is to generate a sense of accomplishment as you complete each step. This step will provide you with the added energy you'll need to propel you through the next step. Smaller steps help you get to a point of accomplishment more quickly. Also, it's a good idea to reward yourself after completing each step of the plan—even if it's just dinner out, a shopping excursion, or a round of golf.

A visual display, such as a graph or checklist drawn on a large easel board, helps you track your progress. Your display serves as a reminder and an encouraging barometer of what you are in the process of accomplishing.

Make Careful Estimates

It's important that you do your best to guesstimate how much time, money, and effort you'll need to expend to achieve each step in your action plan. If something is going to be tough, don't delude yourself by assuming that finishing that step will be "a piece of cake."

Suppose you run a medical billing service, and your goal for 2002 is to develop seven new accounts while retaining all existing ones. Based on your experience, you estimate that to get one new client, you'll need to make three high-quality sales presentations. And you figure it will take five phone calls to get just one appointment. Also, you have been averaging three leads per networking event.

So your action plan could look like this:

- Goals for the year: Seven new clients.
- Sales presentations needed to achieve this goal: 21 (3 x 7).
- Phone calls needed: 107 (21 x 5).
- Networking events to attend: 35 (x 3 @ each = 105).

To summarize, it will take you 35 networking events to get 105 leads to call upon by phone, and out of that volley of calls you will be able to set up 21 presentations, which ought to net you your 7 new clients.

- Breaking this down into monthly objectives (dividing by 12), gives you the following:
- About three networking events per month (2.92).
- Fewer than nine calls per month (8.75).
- Under two sales presentations per month (1.75).

Perhaps your goal does not relate directly to sales. You may simply be trying to upgrade your systems to do everything you currently do in a more efficient fashion.

The system described above will still work. Just define the steps needed to achieve your goal, then break them down further until each step is do-able for you. Work backward from your ultimate goal to where you are right now. In other words, ask yourself, "How do I get from Point A to

Point B? What must happen before I reach my ultimate goal?"

Remember: Take your trek to the mountaintop in manageable stretches of trail. Don't forget to rest after you've negotiated a tough stretch—and reward yourself along the way!

Do not be too timid and squeamish about your actions. All life is an experiment.

— Ralph Waldo Emerson

The ultimate measure of a man is not where he stands in moments of comfort, but where he stands at times of challenge and controversy.

— Martin Luther King, Jr.

The great thing in this world is not so much where we are going but in what direction we are moving.

— Oliver Wendell Holmes

Try not. Do or do not. There is no try.

— Yoda ("*Star Wars*")

CHAPTER 8

Setting Goals is GREAT— Now, How Do You Attain Them?

Keeping Your Business on Track

Results! Why, man, I have gotten a lot of results.
I know several thousand things that won't work.

— Thomas A. Edison

You know your goals. You've set them carefully, and you've even written them down. Let's say, for instance, that you aim to generate ten new accounts over the next three months. You have a good plan and you know where you need to be focused, such as revising your advertising or contacting at least 30 prospects and setting up appointments.

And yet. . . And yet. . . ! There you are fighting brush fires—a thousand interruptions and unexpected setbacks —and you're procrastinating on the appointments quest. You're off track—badly! How did this happen? And how can you keep it from happening again?

The solution to your dilemma can be as simple as 1-2-3 (but let's distinguish "simple" from "simplistic" or "easy." Training well to run a good marathon is simple: Run every day and cover progressively longer distances. But that doesn't mean it's easy to do.) Let me now give you three basic steps for keeping your business (and yourself) on track.

Measure Your Own Progress

Develop a Key Measure. A key measure is any technique or method that can translate into a number or a statistic you can track. This will allow you to gauge just how much you are focused and moving ahead on your plan—or how much you have fallen behind and need to catch up.

For consultants or anyone in a service organization, a good key measure is face-to-face or phone conversations about your business. You can't add clients without talking to prospects about what you have to offer. So simply keeping a running tally of the people to whom you present your service is very, very useful.

Or let's take advertising for a clothing store. Perhaps the store has so far done only point-of-purchase advertising interior sale notices. Now this independent retailer wants to go head-to-head with the department stores in weekly or even daily newspapers. Frequently, the reason people bog down on launching a new ad campaign is that they haven't learned to break the advertising process down into definable steps that can be checked off as each is accomplished. These steps typically include

1. choosing a product to promote,

2. looking into the possible ways to advertise that product and selecting one,

3. designing an ad-copy and illustration,

4. researching and buying the best print space or air time to increase traffic into your store, and

5. tracking customers generated specifically by your ad through such tools as coupons returned or informal inquiries.

By isolating each stage of the advertising project, you will find you are much more likely to stay focused and achieve the result of increased customer flow.

Usually small business owners are tempted to try to track revenues or net income as their key measure. But there's a problem here. While such monitoring is necessary for the overall health of your business, it does very little toward keeping you focused or on track. The reason is that there's too much delay between your day-to-day actions and the shifts in revenues or net income. You need something that is much closer to your daily activities.

To illustrate a bit in another economic sector, restaurants are especially prone to want to gauge their success, or lack of it, by daily receipts. But such receipts, especially for newer restaurants, may not adequately reflect customer satisfaction. Many people will try a restaurant in its first year or so of existence. But are they coming back again and again, as you'd like them to?

What you might really want to track is repeat business. Such tracking, however, is either awkward—actually asking people if they are repeat customers—or time consuming. Tips, however, do serve as a direct reflection of customers' satisfaction with the overall quality of the restaurant, including food, service, and atmosphere. And they are much easier to track than repeat business. So tips do fit the description of an ideal key measure.

Take Advantage of Graphs and Charts

Design a Visual Display. This will be a graphic representation of your key measure or of anything else that is important to track. The easiest example here is one that just about everyone has seen; it's the thermometer set up in the town square to show the amount of money raised at a given time for a community project—and the amount still needed.

Every good visual display will incorporate the three

elements shown in the thermometer example: the current status of your project, the goal to be achieved, and an implicit call to action.

A to-do list is a simple visual display and one that you're probably already using. It shows what's done and what's yet undone. And it calls for action, doesn't it?

Graphs are good, too, especially if you use different color markers. You can graph your new customers, graph coupons returned, graph the progress on the marketing of your various product lines, and graph the dollar volume of sales.

Let's say you're working at home now but you have a goal of developing an office in a commercial space. Even though you cannot afford the space yet, you might work up a visual display of an office floor plan. Then post the drawings in a prominent place at home. You'll be constantly spurred to generate the capital you'll need to accomplish the move.

A common visual display for people working on complex projects, such as constructing a house or a commercial building, is called a "Gantt chart." Along the bottom of such a chart you run a time line for the whole project, from start to finish. Along the left-hand margin, you put the major components, such as "foundation," "sewer," "frame," "roof," "plumbing," and "electricity." These steps have to be accomplished in a certain sequence if the project is to be handled expeditiously and turn out right (just try to put in sewer lines, for instance, after you've poured the concrete foundation).

Such a display can work well for any number of businesses that have to manage complex projects or else many projects at once.

Project management boards can tell you at a glance the status of each of several projects that are moving along concurrently. This is tremendously useful for people who have to jump from one project to another through a series of phone calls, memos, or letters.

Thus Gantt and similar charts show you where you are in a given project and what still needs to happen and in what order.

Lend a Willing Ear

A Committed Listener. This is a person to whom you can explain and report on your key measure, your visual display, or the status of your projects or your progress toward goals. Pick someone outside your business, NOT a colleague, client, or employee. You want someone with a bit of distance from your everyday struggles. While a spouse is a possible choice, be careful here: You're going to add another level to a relationship that is already daunting and complex enough. So whom can you choose?

Good friends make excellent committed listeners. So can fellow members of an Exchange Club, Jaycee group or chamber of commerce.

If you happen to be paying a consultant to help you guide your business growth, he or she absolutely should be functioning as a committed listener. This is a natural role for consultants.

What else should you look for in a committed listener? Two things, above all else:

- Someone who listens very, very well, and
- Someone who is able to resist from swamping you with "you shoulds" and "you shouldn'ts."

The role is called "a committed listener" for a reason—you want the person to do much more listening than advising. The ideal is for you to be able to think things through while talking out loud and gradually work out your own best solutions.

Put another way, you want to work with someone who doesn't have the emotional attachments to your business that you do, who can be more detached or rational and simply get you to tell him or her—and in the process, yourself—the score.

One of the main reasons to have a committed listener is so you can make promises to an actual person, not just to yourself, about what you plan to accomplish during a given time frame. Your next report, then, to your Listener should go something like this: "I promised to collect three overdue accounts, and I managed to get partial payments from two." Then you would make a promise to your listener for the next period.

It's good for your committed listener to be "programmed" to acknowledge your day-to-day accomplishments. Frequently, it's the little things that move your business forward and that need to be recognized. When we're in the middle of running a business, we all too often discount those little things (such as an ad campaign successfully launched or traffic flow increased by 10 percent).

On the other hand, you won't need any stern reminders of the negatives. The downsides shown by your key measure will be plenty apparent to you.

Your committed listener should refrain from indulging in any blaming or shaming. Rather, the person might ask you to explain why something didn't work or what got you off track. These are useful questions.

A final suggestion: It works quite nicely to pick a committed listener who also needs you to function as a committed listener for him or her. Pairing off with someone in a non-competitive sector is an excellent idea and might be key to long-term success for both of you.

Increase Your Productivity with Good Time Management

Life is to be lived. If you have to support yourself, you had
bloody well better find some way that is going to be interesting.
And you don't do that by sitting around wondering about yourself.

— Katharine Hepburn

When you had a salaried job, you may have had to put some energy into "looking busy." Remember those times when there was really nothing to do on your watch, but a supervisor would occasionally "check in" on you anyway? You always kept a nice stack of forms or correspondence ready to pull over the travel magazine you were reading, right? The trick was to time the shift so that the supervisor wouldn't notice what you were covering up.

Now that you're on your own as an entrepreneur, you have to check up on yourself. No one is going to. Instead of merely looking busy, you find that to survive you actually have to be busy.

Never make the mistake, however, of confusing motion with progress, or "busyness" with "business." Unless you learn how to work smart, all of your rushing around in six different directions may lead only to the collapse of your endeavor.

So, let's spend a few moments looking at what has been euphemistically called "time management." First, a small caveat: "Time management" is obviously a misnomer. We cannot manage time; it will not obey our efforts to whip it into line, but will pursue its relentless course, second by second, minute by minute, like sand dropping through an hourglass. All we can manage is ourselves, our own thoughts and actions. Just to speak in the popular idiom, however, we'll go ahead and use the term "time management" in this discussion.

Focus Is the Key to Getting Things Done

Have you ever noticed that the more focused you are on something, the more efficiently you can work through a project to a successful conclusion? By staying focused and not allowing ourselves to get sidetracked by other concerns, we produce more, and higher quality, results. What can we do to achieve this focus?

First and above all, know yourself as deeply as you possibly can. Are you a "morning person" or an "afternoon-evening" person? If your biorhythms are such that you typically drone through early morning in a semi-comatose state, try to arrange your day from, say, 10 a.m. to 6 p.m. Conversely, morning people may do better to start work at around 6 a.m. and wind down by 2 p.m. (Such scheduling is not always possible, or course, because we all have other constraints, but when it is, it is very useful to go with the flow of your individual biorhythms.)

Do you work best in relative solitude? Then working at home might be your work-style of choice, or, if you work in an office, you may want to be sufficiently walled off from others to protect yourself from undue noise, interruptions, or chatter.

On the other hand, if you happen to be a groupie, you might find yourself spinning your wheels in non-productive busyness working at home alone; recognize that you actually need to be in other people's company to be your productive best. If this is your style, a shared office suite might be better for you. Find your own personal match, and then go with it!

Are you something of a procrastinator by nature? A perfectionist? A chatterbox? For each of these types there are definitive downsides—and ways to counter such minuses.

My best advice for people saddled with a bent for procrastinating is simply to start on a project—anywhere. Dive into the middle of it, start at the fringes, start with the most attractive feature of it, but start! Do something, anything. Once you are in action, you'll find that you have released a lot of energy that will quite likely carry you through to the end. It is really the process of agonizing over how we "should" do something that drains our energy. Such worrying robs us of the focus we need to be truly productive.

If the reason behind your procrastination is that a particular project appears overwhelming to you, break it up into manageable pieces. For instance, completing a business plan aimed at raising a half a million dollars is indeed a formidable undertaking. Who wouldn't balk at diving in? What if, however, you developed a pool of entrepreneurs and helped provide input and feedback on each other's plans? Then, taking it one section at a time and perhaps blocking our extended meetings over five weeks, you would be able to help each other through the drafting of your respective plans. Community colleges, business centers, and SCORE executives are also marvelous resources for leading people through the drafting of their business plans. Pick up the phone and make a call. Don't let such valuable resources go untapped!

Aids to Keep You Moving Along

"To do" lists—however you choose to structure them— are invaluable aids to staying focused. Some people like to type the next day's "to do" list on their computer. Others may jot it down in a notebook or planner or post it on an oversized calendar above their desk. Do whatever works for you, but find something that works.

Setting priorities is usually a necessity. You should certainly prepare your "to do" list for the day—but also rank things in 1-2-3 order according to what's most critical. Here too, knowing your own personality and its corresponding work style is important. There are those who say that unless you get No. 1 wrapped up, don't even dream of going on to No. 2. Other people I know counter, no, no, no! You always have to keep several projects moving along simultaneously. How about you? What's your style? Are you a one-thing-at-a-time person? Or a juggler?

The Bane of Perfectionism

Perfectionists may have different problems from the typical procrastinator (although there's a way in which it is possible to do both). If you're a perfectionist, a job can never be called "finished," because you never do get to "perfect." Stephanie Winston, in her book *The Organized Executive*, describes perfectionism as "a compulsive striving for an ideal of excellence or 'organization' far beyond any utilitarian purpose." An example would be retyping an inter-office memo just because there were a couple of punctuation marks out of place.

There is a high level of quality consciousness operating

now in corporate America, and small businesses are smart to try to fit in. Nonetheless, for every project or effort there comes a point of diminishing returns, when striving for more quality than is actually called for causes you to miss a deadline or irritates a client or shortchanges another project of equal importance. Your perfectionism could spell failure instead of success for your products or services.

Monitor yourself (or ask a friend to do it) to find out whether you are a gusher of words instead of someone who chooses to aim those words carefully. If you can economize on your communications without, of course, sacrificing anything to clarity, you will have more time and energy to focus on other actions. Also, colleagues, clients, suppliers and others will appreciate your brevity. Don't forget: They too have things they must focus upon. It's good to know when you have said enough and heard enough and how to politely end a conversation, whether face-to-face or over the phone.

A Few Closing Tips

Handling interruptions. Once again, almost everybody has a different favorite approach. Learning to say "no" in one form or another is universally useful. Some entrepreneurs may rule out taking incoming calls until a given project is finished. Or they insist on solitude for a daily meditation period. Just remember that there are times when you need to let an interruption override what you're working on. Some examples: A major client has an emergency and needs your attention. An employee gets sick or injured and has to be driven to the doctor's office or hospital. An ad for a product you've been searching for pops out at you and today is the deadline for the distributor's 50% off sale. And so on.

Order and atmosphere. It goes without saying—but we need to be remind ourselves of it anyway—that people who can put and keep things in order normally make better use of their working hours than those who cannot. Very little time is ever spent tracking down a file or letter because it's right there where you filed it. And if you need a paper clip or Scotch tape or a memo pad, viola! They're all within reach. Also, if your workspace is decorated in a fashion that's relaxing or pleasing to you, you'll be much more "up" for toiling away there, even at the most menial task. Good lighting and perhaps a view of greenery or even an interesting facade across the street may help too. Finally, many people work better to background music. If you are one of them, make sure you treat yourself to it.

Pause between projects. When you complete a job, stop and acknowledge the accomplishment. Spend a moment to check it off your to-do list before you move on. You'd be surprised at how much this simple act can restore your energy level.

Another valuable technique is to take a mini-vacation from your work as you finish one job and before you move on to the next. It could be anything from fetching a fresh cup of coffee to closing your eyes and doing nothing but listening to music for a few minutes. You'll typically experience a recharging of your batteries, a new flow of energy; in this way you'll be better able to refocus your attention or shift gears for the next job you'll be tackling.

CHAPTER

10

Turn Your Work Life Around

Achieving Good Organization

Discipline is remembering what you want.

— David Campbell

I would bet that nine out of ten people starting to read this chapter want or need help in getting organized. And eight out of those nine are already cringing in fear of what they think will be a painful disjunction of their personality or lifestyle.

On the other hand, dollars and (good) sense are at issue here if you hope to achieve your potential for success as an entrepreneur. So latch on to any familiar, comforting slogan you like—"no pain, no gain," "there's no free lunch," "nothing ventured, nothing gained," and so on—and let's get battle-ready to defeat the dragon of disorganization once and for all.

It's true that some people have a natural bent for organization. One friend's twelve-year-old daughter seems to have been born with a gift for order. Her room is as neat as a pin; everything is in its place. Her school notebooks are models of readability and completeness. Nobody ever taught her to do it that way. In fact, her parents are notably less organized than she is.

Experience has shown me, however, that most of us find ourselves struggling with heaps of paperwork, invoices and receipts buried in the wrong files, desks spilling over with scraps and scribblings and marginally useful pamphlets and printouts. We also tend to lose important documents and even fail to jot down our expenses or remember all our appointments. Is there hope that we can achieve real and lasting change?

Yes! You can do it! It will take commitment, will power, discipline, and a hefty dose of persistence. Know, nonetheless, that plenty of others have made the switch from chaos to productive organization, and that includes people who were just as "hopeless" as you when they started their change program.

The Tangible Benefits

Whatever the reason for your lack of organization, the benefits that will accrue to you as you move through your change process are stunningly impressive. You will be considerably more productive and consequently more successful at whatever you undertake. This will result in much less stress and frustration. You'll be able to enjoy life more and accomplish much more with your talents and energy.

Clients and customers naturally gravitate to people who display good organization because organized people typically are very reassuring to those who seek to spend their money wisely and well.

Organized people inevitably convey a more professional image. After all, rustling around your office for ten minutes to locate a file of concern to a client who has called on you in person does not inspire much confidence. And you will have wasted twenty minutes of working time: ten minutes of yours and ten of your client's.

Systems Must Meet Your Goals

The first principle of organization is to design all systems to meet your goals.

The details of organization will vary somewhat from person to person, company to company. What may be of great importance to you—such as always paying bills by the 30th of the month—may be less so to someone else.

If your goals are too vague, you must first clarify them. Sit yourself down for a good long working session of goals-charting. When you are finished, be sure to write out these goals. Otherwise, how in the world are you going to get organized to meet something that isn't clear even to the Number One beneficiary of the whole exercise?

There isn't room in this chapter for an extended discussion of goals setting. But if you need immediate help, I suggest you borrow or purchase *Goal Setting*, by Susan B. Wilson and read it carefully. Then continue with this article. For those whose goals are sufficiently clear already, we'll go on.

A few examples of organization to meet goals:

An independent sales rep whose stock-in-trade rides in his car along with him must put a high premium on organizing his traveling files and being sure that essential items such as samples, agendas, and order forms are always right at hand. Perhaps he can allow himself to get a bit behind with his office or home filing, but not with what goes in the car.

A restaurant owner cannot afford to run low on inventory likely to be in high demand. If her main items are burgers and fish plates, she had better lay lots of ketchup and tartar sauce on hand. Running out of either of these is sure to anger and perhaps drive away patrons who take such accouterments for granted.

A public relations consultant trying to sell her services to one of the Midwest's biggest public corporations absolutely must have a wardrobe of classic suits and a nick-free genuine leather briefcase. Her hair and makeup must also have the polished look expected of women in high-power positions. Whatever it takes to achieve this look must always be in perfect order.

A good overall principle of organization is accessibility.

You must always be able to lay your hands on the essential components of whatever you need to perform your service or produce your product efficiently—and do it in no time flat. For most of us, this usually includes (but is certainly not limited to

- a reliable computer,
- neatly organized diskettes,
- a decent printer with paper close at hand and ready to go,
- telephone answering machine,
- the whole range of office supplies (pens, pencils, erasers, paper clips, clear tape, pushpins, scissors, memo pads and so on).

Your all-important files should include:

- dossiers on all active clients,
- inventory files,
- financial records,
- networking or customer-base files.

You should also have close at hand important reference works for your sector, whether in book or on-line form.

Check today (before the spirit of reform departs) to see what needs restocking, refurbishing, renewing, reorganizing, or acquiring. Write down your findings and post them on the wall over your work area. Resolve that you will not rest content until everything that needs doing has been done.

Here's another vital principle you can tack up on your bulletin board: Do not flinch from spending both time and money on organization. Any effort worth doing will take both. You will have to take some time away from other endeavors to create and maintain effective systems, but the rewards will be worth it. And you will almost certainly have to spend money for an effective computer system, file cabinets and folders, and the full range of office supplies.

Don't just think it over. Do it.

Use Whatever Works for You

When you are designing your systems, remember that virtually any system will work if you work it properly. So design something that is user-friendly for you. If you're not comfortable with your systems, how long do you think you'll keep them up? Some people love computerized personal organizers; others find them a pain and stick to a calendar, an address book, and a pencil. There is no point to setting up a whiz-bang system if you don't like using it. It's often best to keep things as simple as possible.

Take advantage of the many products available to help keep you organized and on track. These include desktop sorters, stacking trays, colorful, easy-to-use labels, and many more. Your office supply store—or their catalog—can offer guidance. Don't be penny-wise in this area if it means being pound-foolish in your net receipts.

And for heaven's sake, get yourself a practical and attractive desk, one that gives you all the room you need to spread out manuals and files and do your paperwork. Do keep in mind that your desk is not meant to replace your file cabinets. Don't use it as a storage locker. When you have finished one project, scoop all the paperwork and deposit it neatly back into your very efficient filing system before you dive into the next project.

Nothing impedes productivity more than letting papers accumulate on your desk and take up residence there.

Every piece of paper you touch should either be filed or thrown away. I know this is a tough one for all us pack rats (and I say "us" because I'm afflicted with this malady myself). Lisa Kanarek, in her book *Organizing Your Home Office for Success*, lists these reasons that people insist on keeping stacks of paper on the desk or floor:

• They haven't made a decision about each piece of paper.

• They want to remind themselves of the tasks they need to accomplish.

• They're afraid of filing a piece of paper and never seeing it again.

• They don't have a specific place to put a given piece of paper.

• They want to keep a document around "just in case."

Whatever your reason, cut through it decisively and adhere to the file-or-toss rule. When in doubt, save tax, legal, or business items and deep-six informational items that you seldom, if ever, use.

Filing for Success

You know your business better than anyone else. So you are the best expert to determine the categories you want to capture on file labels. Just the same, I'd like to throw in a few suggestions from systems I've come upon in my work as a financial consultant.

I especially like one system that had stacking bins labeled "To Sort," "To Read," "To Do," "To File," and "Errands." That seemed to me to cover all the bases for papers still hovering around the desk area.

Some filing systems are divided into "Current," "Historical" and "Reference" categories. Current houses anything that is ongoing with any of your clients or prospects. Historical includes past clients and projects. Reference is research material that may apply to any aspect of your operation but is probably targeted to things still on the horizon.

For my own financial recordkeeping, I use the following categories: Clients/Projects, Unpaid Bills, Paid Bills, Unpaid Invoices, Paid Invoices, and Business Expenses and Equipment.

It's best to sort items just arrived on your desk into piles, using the categories above or other categories specific to your business. Sometimes it's easier to do this, at least for the first time, with a friend, colleague, or employee close at hand. If the other person has a natural bent for organization, you'll find his or her presence a big plus. Once you have all the papers sorted, get them into existing or new files for their category and PUT THE FILE FOLDER INTO THE CABINET. It is tempting to keep these folders on top of your desk where you can actually see them, but for those tempted, I have just one word of advice: DON'T.

Staying Organized

Once you have gotten yourself well-organized, your next goal is to stay that way. To do this, acquire and read good books on getting organized. Some good ones include

• *Organized to be the Best*, 2nd ed., by Susan Silver (Adams-Hall Publishing, 1991).

- *Organizing Your Home Office for Success*, by Lisa Kanarek (Penguin Books, 1993).
- *The Organized Executive*, by Stephanie Winston (Warner Books, 1985).

Also, cultivate people who seem to have a gift for organization. Finally, make a weekly appointment with yourself to review the state of your organizing efforts. Count on putting in real effort each time this appointment rolls around. After awhile, it will all seem as natural as brushing your teeth in the morning. And you'll be glad, very glad, that you made the switch.

Take what you can use and let the rest go by.

— Ken Kesey

Business is a process of diverting one's scattered forces into one powerful channel.

— James Allen

Look at a day when you are supremely satisfied at the end. It's not a day when you lounge around doing nothing; it's when you've had everything to do, and you've done it.

— Margaret Thatcher

Just do it.

— Nike Corporation ad

Section IV

BUSINESS DEVELOPMENT

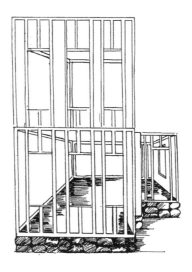

BUILD YOUR BUSINESS STRONGER—

CHAPTER

11

Get a Great Profit Picture

Edit Your Business Like a Movie

You have to know what you want to get it.

— Gertrude Stein

Script writers, directors, and especially film editors are very conscious of what it takes to make a great movie: An astute and happy blending of three kinds of shots—close-ups, medium shots, and long shots. Each kind has its own distinct purpose. Nonetheless, the three shots must work together to reinforce each other.

If any single shot dominates, it is probably the medium shot—not the tight focus on a hand reaching for the telephone, nor the panorama of a cityscape or beach, but the shot that includes the interaction of two or three people with some evidence of a physical context (office, home, restaurant, wherever).

This is a good lesson for those of us starting, or building, a business.

Let's look at these three shots, as they apply to tracking what's going on with your business.

The Close-up

This is the short-range view. It offers a lot of detail about a small part of the business, such as monthly or quarterly financial reports, which show cash flow, debt reduction, inventory, payroll, and profit or loss. Your accountant is likely to take this view of your business.

In addition to financials, you might think of short-range views of other systems:

• Your marketing package (where and how you advertise or do other promotions and what results the effort seems to be generating).

• Your employee policies and relations (how people are translating your hopes for growth into action, as well as how they are meshing with one another as they carry out their jobs), your product development (is it stagnant? Or, at the other extreme, overly ambitious and chaotic?).

People who are good at detail love this perspective. These are the folks who won't let anything fall through the cracks. If something appears to be out of place, they'll identify it and try to set it straight. A secretary or executive assistant who takes this view is worth his or her weight in gold.

The short-range view, or close-up, is critical for the effective day-to-day operation of your business. It is ideal for marshaling and studying the facts—especially the numbers—that tell you how you are doing. It's also vital for making sure you're not overlooking any essential ingredient for success.

Limiting yourself to a short-range view, however, will get you bogged down in details instead of making the important decisions that will help you reach your potential. People who get stuck in the short range are constantly poring over the facts. Often these folks tell themselves, "If I just get every single little detail in place, then I'll see the bigger picture and be able to move things forward." Usually this is a delusion. To truly move a business forward, the owner or manager needs to let go of the short-range or close-up view and move on to the Big Picture.

The Big Picture

This is the long-range view. It's about looking out over the horizon and pointing to a Shangri-La or Bali Hai glimpsed in the hazy distance and proclaiming, "I'm going there!"

The big-picture view is directly opposite the short-range perspective. This is the view of visionaries and futurists. If you notice businesses around you that haven't grown much in five or ten years, businesses that seem to be complacent and stuck in a routine, you can bet that they haven't been marching toward anything on the horizon. Their focus has been limited to the day-to-day or short-term view.

People capable of seeing the big picture know how to create a dream and sell others on bringing that dream into reality. They are like explorers standing on the bow of a boat, looking through a spyglass and searching the distance for the promised land.

Steve Jobs of Apple and Bill Gates of Microsoft provide excellent examples of big-picture visionaries. They both saw emerging industries long before most others did. Their seeing something that escaped the notice of competitors gave them the ultimate edge and propelled their companies to dynamic success.

Nothing builds team spirit like having a vision. In his book *The Fifth Discipline*, Peter Senge, director of MIT's Systems Thinking and Organizational Development Program, lists "shared vision" as a core principle of success. What he means is not only developing the vision among the top few people at a firm, but also managing to communicate that vision so that all employees catch the fire. When a company team is heading in the same direction like a Roman phalanx, the competition had better look out!

Robert Fritz, a friend of Senge's and author of *The Path of Least Resistance*, cites vision as one of two key ingredients of his model of "structural tension," which he outlines in a recent book, *Corporate Tides*. As Fritz defines it, structural tension provokes a tendency for a company to move in a certain direction. When it is properly applied, this tension will pull you and your people like a rubber band toward your purpose or goal. This is vision in action.

Like the short-range view, however, big-picture thinking has a drawback: If you stay fixated on the long-range, you will miss the details of what's happening in the day-to-day world. Anyone who remains stuck in the big picture is likely to be taken for a starry-eyed dreamer who does not have his or her feet on the ground. So indulge yourself in healthy doses of blue-sky visioning, but practice the art of coming back to the concrete reality of the here and now.

A Middle Course

In between the long- and short-range views is, obviously, the medium-range view—not too close and not too far off. Like the baby bear's porridge that Goldilocks finds to her liking, it's "neither too hot nor too cold, but just right."

This view is perfect for understanding patterns in our worklife, such as problems with time management or work flow, and for spotting trends in our own section of the marketplace. Such business patterns and trends give us much of the useful information we need to make good decisions on financing, strategizing, and marketing.

All business strategy comes down to matching you and your endeavor with market conditions. Doing this is difficult, if not impossible, if you can't clearly see the overall trends, a function of adopting a middle-range perspective.

Senge states in *The Fifth Discipline* that "Today, our primary threat to survival, both (for) our organizations and (for) our societies, comes not from sudden events but from slow, gradual processes."

Let's recall that the Japanese automakers' share of the American car market was below 5 percent in 1962. The Big Three U.S. manufacturers scarcely noticed when this share quietly climbed to just under 10 percent by 1967. Not until the early 1980s, when the Japanese share had risen to 21.3 percent, did Detroit really wake up and start to pay attention. Late reactions by Ford, Chrysler, and General Motors proved inadequate, however, to hold back the Japanese assault on the market. By 1989, the Japanese share had climbed to 30 percent!

The U.S. automakers had been too preoccupied with both the short-range view of their year-to-year operations, and the long-range vision of how their dazzling cars of the future would perform on automated highways, to focus on the middle range. And that helps explain the phenomenal success of the Japanese imports.

The middle range is also great for training your people for market challenges that are just around the corner or for conceptualizing an advertising campaign that you want to last three or four years. It's the range your banker wants to help you think in as he or she charts your growth projections and tries to get you to situate yourself in the context of ongoing market forces.

Being tied to any one viewpoint is always limiting. But if you had to adapt to just one viewpoint of the three available to you, the middle view would be the most practical. It offers enough of a balanced perspective so that you can see the details and also glimpse the bigger picture.

Summing Up

Now that you have some understanding of each of the three perspectives for looking at your business, ask yourself: Which of these views do I spend most of my time looking at my business with? Am I capable of using each of the three when necessary? Is there any of the three that I have not developed at all? The answers to these questions will shed some light on the way you've been running your venture.

Where you discover a weak spot, try to shore it up. If you are, for example, virtually unable to look through the long-range lens, find another business person who has that capability and see if you can learn from him or her. Using all three viewpoints—and knowing how to shift back and forth as circumstances may demand—will help you reap tremendous rewards for your business.

If you'd like more details on this concept, I highly recommend Robert Fritz's book, *Corporate Tides* (Berrett-Koehler, 1996).

Nothing contributes so much to tranquilizing the mind as a steady purpose—a point on which the soul may fix its intellectual eye.

— Mary Wollstonecraft Shelley

I had no ambition to make a fortune. Mere money-making has never been my goal. I had an ambition to build.

— John D. Rockefeller, Jr.

CHAPTER 12

Know Where Your Business Is Right Now

Recognize the Stages in Business Growth

When one door closes another door opens; but we often look so long and so regretfully upon the closed door that we do not see the one which opens for us.

— Alexander Graham Bell

To succeed in business, you need what? A great product or service, consumer demand, a super location, the "right" people to work with you or for you, adequate capitalization, a marketing plan, a vision of where you want to go with your venture. . . and. . . and. . . ? Is there anything more?

Yes, there is. You need a clear understanding that business grows by stages. Not only that, but the stages are different, one from another, in how they will challenge you and what it will take to conquer each challenge. In other words, the mindsets and skills that will help you scale the first peak on your climb toward entrepreneurial success may not be good enough to get you up to the summit during the next stage.

Frightening? It certainly can be. The toughest part, however, is when you don't even realize that these stages exist, nor how each stage is constituted and the challenges each provokes, nor when and how to move from one stage to the next.

Entrepreneurs (meaning, here, anyone who starts a business of any size) typically picture a smooth growth curve, ascending sales, increasing revenues. It all sounds wonderful. The real world, though, frequently does not cooperate by fulfilling that vision. There are usually false starts, unexpected hurdles, setbacks, and dilemmas along the way.

Stage One—Formulation

Take John Whitstone. Like many entrepreneurs, John—who launched a computer consulting business—has been able to weather the rough start-up stage. He has a downtown office, a burgeoning client base and a number of key systems in place (files, marketing brochure, a networking group on Thursday mornings). Somehow, however, the revenues have not been what John had expected. He is just "getting by." And he is unsure how to build a more prosperous enterprise.

John has come through the formulation and early growth stage. And this stage has played into his creative bent. He has had to invent much of what he had to sell and has had to prospect—hard—for clients. Because he was not clear on what services would bring in the most money, John has tried a bit of everything: Web site design, troubleshooting to solve systems problems, brokering new equipment and upgrades, training people on the latest software programs, and so on. In short, he has been inventing his business as he went along. Experimenting with a number of products fits well with the early growth stage, say the first two or three years.

But then it's time to move on!

Stage Two—Management

Consolidating your strengths and solidifying your potential for growth mandates a different approach. In this important growth stage, you should focus on putting in place the structures to transform your startup into a true contender for long-term success. In other words, you need to become a company with staying power, able to defend yourself against the competition and keep on track for steady growth. This is not easy.

Whereas John survived the startup stage with pluck, entrepreneurial zeal, creativity, enthusiastic salesmanship, and the delivery of satisfactory products, he will need something different to succeed in Stage Two: Management! Stage Two will probably involve strengthening the business plan and winning a higher line of credit or investor backing, taking on employees and training them to keep and expand the customer base by providing quality service, and, inevitably, dancing through the maze of more involvement in tracking and planning by your CPA, your banker and your legal advisors. There are issues of incorporation, insurance, liability, and more to contend with.

In terms of products, rather than continuing with scattershot experiment, trying to be all things to all customers, the key to success in Stage Two will be selecting what you do best and eliminating areas where you are the weakest. You should be carving out a niche, in other words a niche where you are at or near the top of the competition. In this stage, trying to hold onto all of your services and products will, in most instances, be an obstacle to your success. Specialize in what you do well.

While John was in the startup, or formulation, stage, he was able to try many different approaches to developing products. There appeared to be few rules or constraints—in short, he had a lot of flexibility. He had website customers, troubleshooting customers, and software training customers. He floated from one service to the next, enjoying the variety as his adrenaline pumped him through the day.

Creative types who live on spontaneous challenges and who prefer an open-ended or unstructured environment usually love the startup stage. These same people can quickly flounder when faced with the demands of the consolidation stage, however, and unless they undergo a raw radical change of mindset or bring in the right person to help, the business can go down in flames right there.

A management mindset will eliminate the marginally profitable products and highlight the high-demand products that bring in the most revenue. Management means taking something that has worked well and institutionalizing it—doing it over and over again, fine tuning it as you go and training your people to do it just as well as you.

Returning to John, our computer consultant, we now find that John has hired a business coach to help him with decisions. Analyzing what worked best has led to the conclusion that he should focus on networking computer systems integrating, getting the glitches out, coordinating with printers and scanners and so on. The idea now is to take this strength and make it into a mainstay for years and years to come. John will then become known as "the best there is" in this area, and demand for the services of his company will remain strong.

The major characteristic of the growth stage is repetition: Doing a smaller set of operations than before and doing them over and over. As you can imagine, this is hard for many entrepreneurs. They see this sort of routinizing of their operations as boring. They may also find it hard to cope with another requirement of Stage Two: scrupulous record keeping. Without such records, it is impossible to track things, to know how your sales and your expenses are going. Without records, it is difficult to make informed decisions. And without informed decisions, well, you can just imagine what will happen to John's enterprise—or yours!

During Stage Two the entrepreneur should invest his or her creativity in making improvements—fine-tuning the operations that the company has decided to keep. This is the time for total quality management, management by objectives, and just-in-time inventory management.

In this culture, variations on the tried and true will reward you and your company. You will have to limit yourself to services or products that have proven their worth and reject many fresh—even worthwhile—ideas for other products.

Stage Three—Innovation

This will bring back a focus on innovation. In fact, I call it the Innovation Stage. You will be on the cusp of Stage Three when your company, after getting all your operations down to a regular routine and becoming solidly profitable, finds nonetheless that it is losing market share. The competition, in other words, has encroached on what you have built; as the saying goes, "They are gaining on you." To outpace the competition you need to stop relying on simply the routines that worked well in Stage Two. You will, indeed, need to dip back into the creative mode of Stage One—come up with noticeable refinements in your existing products, and very likely develop entirely new products. You may even want to revisit ideas that you rejected or put on hold while you were perfecting your act in Stage Two.

Now that you recognize that there are different, identifiable stages in the evolution of a business, you need to ask yourself: Where am I right now? In the middle of Stage One (startup, formulation)? Getting close to the jumping off point for Stage Two? Where? Honest questioning will give you a head start.

Recognizing the Transitions

Then it's important to understand just what it takes to move from one stage to the next. The biggest clue to knowing when it is time to move is when you see that what has worked for you in the past is no longer working so well. You are doing all the same things that brought you success, but it becomes like butting your head against a wall. You sense that you must do something different to move your venture forward. And you are right.

Making the shift involves not only changing your way of doing business, but also changing your mental models and ways of behaving. This is often harder than changing the nuts and bolts of your operation. As you shift, for example, from the strictly entrepreneurial mindset to the managerial mindset, much will feel strange and uncomfortable.

You may have to review your values and goals. Almost surely, you will have to rewrite your business plan. You may have to find a partner or associate whose mindsets and skills make up for what you may lack. The visionary entrepreneur, for instance, is not always adept at close tracking and budgeting.

In some instances an entrepreneur may decide to draw back from moving into the next stage. If growing your business into a large entity is not your goal, recognize this and go for the growth that fits who you are.

There is nothing wrong with staying small—if that meshes with the income and lifestyle that suits you. On the other hand, if you're trying to grow bigger and you find you are stuck, you may want to re-read this chapter and take notes on what comes up in your mind and your emotions as you read. Your own intuition will be your best guide to telling you where you are now—and what you need to do to take your business to the next level.

Markets change, tastes change, so the companies and the individuals who choose to compete in those markets must change.

— An Wang, founder, Wang Labs

When someone offers you a challenge, don't think of all the reasons why you can't do it. Instead, say "Yes!" Then figure out how you'll get it done.

— Katherine Hudson, President and CEO,
W. H. Brady Co.

I am convinced that if the rate of change inside an organization is less than the rate of change outside, the end is in sight.

— Jack Welch, Chairman and CEO, General Electric

I don't like to repeat success, I like to go on to other things.

— Walt Disney

In life, change is inevitable. In business, change is vital.

    — Warren Bennis

Your work is to discover your work, and then with all your heart to give yourself to it.

    — Buddha

A new idea is first condemned as ridiculous, and then dismissed as trivial, until finally it becomes what everybody knows.

    — William James

Only those who risk going too far can possibly find out how far one can go.

    — T.S. Eliot

CHAPTER 13

Don't Leave Out Anything Important

Six Areas Critical to Growth

Working on your business rather than in your business [must] become the central theme of your daily activity, the prime catalyst for everything you do from this moment forward.

— Michael E. Gerber, **The E-Myth**

Imagine a mobile on your front porch. It has any number of metal and perhaps wooden pieces, all arranged artistically. They fit together in a certain order. If a strong wind comes and jangles the mobile, however, all the pieces move and rearrange themselves, some bumping against the others. If the wind is strong enough, one or more pieces of your mobile may even break off.

Businesses are like that mobile. Various parts such as accounting, personnel, marketing, sales, maintenance, customer service are arranged in particular ways, and interact with each other also in modes determined perhaps by chance development, perhaps by careful planning.

Whenever one part of the businesses undergoes change, however, it quite likely will affect the other parts with which it has been interacting. There's no change in a vacuum—in other words, everything affects everything else.

Right here I would like to highlight six critical areas of

your business that relate to growth, and then invite you to reflect on how they necessarily interact, and on how making a change in any one area will affect all the others. The six areas are 1) technology, 2) information, 3) functions/processes/systems, 4) incentives, 5) competencies, and 6) culture.

Technology

You may not think of your business as very "high tech," but if you look around, you will see that you have surrounded yourself with technology—and depend upon it vitally every day. All electronic programs and the equipment that runs the programs are part of your technology. This includes computers, printers, scanners, fax machines, copiers, your telephone system and equipment, pagers, and any equipment specific to your manufacturing or service business.

It is hard to run any business efficiently these days without technology. And having the right technology can give your business an edge. Why? Because the right technology increases your productivity. It will allow each person who works with you, or for you, to raise the quality or the speed—or both—of the jobs that they do.

Technology, however, is the most unforgiving of the six areas we're looking at here—because it is the least flexible. People usually adapt themselves to technology, not the other way around. How many times haven't you heard someone say, "I can't do that procedure because my computer (or my phone system) won't let me."

In the main, technology is linked to the kinds of information you are trying to manage. Every time you consider making a change in the sort of information you collect or process, you have to ask yourself, "Will our technology allow us to do that? Or do we need to purchase new programs?"

Your business sytems also are inextricably tied up with your technology. By this I mean the way you invoice, the way you take in and process bills from suppliers, the way you manage contacts for current and prospective customers, and even, in some cases, the way you communicate with people in your own organization (pagers, voice mail, cell phones, e-mail, etc.).

Give a lot of thought to how you are "doing" your technology. A failed installation could ruin your business, or, at the least, cause you major headaches. Here are a few questions to help you determine your technological base:

• Is your office currently high tech, medium tech, or low tech? Whichever it is, is your degree of technology appropriate for what you are hoping to accomplish?

• What are the best benefits of your current technology?

• What areas can you identify where your technology needs improvement?

• What would it cost to make those improvements? Can the cost be justified in terms of production or sales advances?

• Are your people willing to be trained to handle a higher level of technological sophistication?

Information

Information is the basis for decisions. It therefore is the means by which you measure what is going on in your business. In other words, an extremely important element.

There are strategic measures such as goals, objectives, business plans, action plans, and change plans. Or financial indices including sales, expenses, salaries, profit, cash flow, growth, and financial strength.

Another information flow tracks things like pending

orders, status of projects/orders, deadlines, resources needed (part), and when the resources are needed. And, finally, there are HR measures. Among these are employee satisfaction, employee competencies, individual motivations, and employee turnover.

Having the right information, and providing the right interpretation, critically determines whether and how your business will grow.

Obviously, information is linked to technology. This is where it's stored, tracked, projected and analyzed. Another area we'll look at shortly, competencies, also comes into play, for technology by itself will just sit there and stare at you. We're still in an age when human beings need to operate the technology and make a judgment on the results of the process.

Managing information wisely is a key to success. We need to understand that information amounts to more than just random data; it is data that comes in a usable form and serves a purpose. That's why consultants design the output (reports) first. What kind of output your business requires should determine the kind of information systems you put in place.

Information supports business decisions. Good information and good interpretation of such feeds right into making wise decisions for your enterprise.

As W. Edwards Deming said, "What you can measure, you can manage."

As a check on your information awareness and management, answer these questions:

• Where are you now in executing your business plan?

• Where does your greatest revenue come from? Your greatest profit?

- How well do you manage operations information? How could you improve?
- What is the current state of employee morale? What would make it better?
- How much information is shared between functions, or departments, of your business?
- How can such sharing be improved?

Functions/systems/processes

Most businesses are organized by functional departments, such as sales, marketing, operations, finance. Within each functional area, systems are set up to generate the work flow. In the main these systems consist of humans interacting with one another and with available technology.

Functions/systems/processes are the most evident part of your business. They are what someone will notice when they walk into your office.

Your systems are generally manifested in, or housed in, your technology. They are part and parcel of your group's competencies—what your business is capable of accomplishing, whether in the manufacture of a product or delivery of a service, or both. Moreover, your own and your employees' skills are channeled through these systems, whether those skills involve accounting, quality control, inventory control, sales, customer service, or something else.

Another element that is interwoven with systems is your company's culture—the "look" and "feel" of how your business operates. Culture is generally created from the top down, although in firms where the principals allow enough freedom, employees too can strongly affect the way culture is created.

Systems and processes need to evolve as the company grows. The systems that served you well when your gross revenues were $100,000 will not hold up when your revenues exceed $1 million. If you do not adjust your systems to match the demands of higher revenue flows and increased workforce, you invite serious problems.

This is the domain of reengineering, work architecture, and process redesign, which frequently means bringing in consultants who are very good in those areas.

Here are a few questions about your systems and processes:

- Can you identify and characterize all the systems currently operating in your business?
- Which are accomplishing their purposes well? Which are falling short?
- How can you make all your systems perform more efficiently?

Competencies

I use this term to indicate the various skills and expertise you and your people have available to run your business. These competencies are strongly determining of success or mediocrity or failure.

The old axiom of General Electric that "people are our most important product" reflects the truth of my assertion.

Competencies in play in your business, or any business, are more numerous than you might realize. In his book *Creating a Culture of Competence*, Michael Zwell, Ph.D., chairman of Zwell International and CEO of Metamorphics lists them according to groups, somewhat as follows:

Individual productivity competencies—
- initiative
- results orientation
- flexibility
- concern for quality
- technical expertise
- personal productivity (getting a lot done)

Personal attribute competencies—
- integrity
- character
- attention to detail
- problem solving
- critical thinking
- innovation/creativity
- emotional intelligence
- personal awareness
- personal development
- interpersonal skills
- high sense of responsibility or accountability

Relationship competencies—
- teamwork skills
- communication skills
- influence or advocacy
- relationship building
- conflict resolution

Managerial competencies—
- corporate goal setting
- decision making
- delegating
- motivating
- giving feedback (praise or criticism)
- monitoring individuals' progress
- building team spirit

Finally, leadership competencies—
- visionary leadership
- strategic thinking
- entrepreneurial thinking
- values and principles
- establishing focus
- communicating vision goals
- building group commitment
- managing change.

There are also industry-specific competencies, such as manual dexterity with instruments or tools, good eye-hand coordination, etc.

Competencies are linked to your company culture. Your culture values certain competencies, and you hire for those. If you are an aware company, you also reward people for their competency, or provide disincentives for not living up to competency.

One way of looking at your business is as an array of competencies. When the level of competency is good from position to position, your company thrives. When that level falls off, your company founders.

To help bring more awareness to yourself and others regarding your business' competencies, respond to the following questions:
- What skill sets are most important to your business?
- What competencies does your company possess that are superior to those of the competition?
- What skill sets have you been only vaguely aware of until now, but which you think you may want to include in your hiring or your staff development?

Incentives

What do you reward in your business? Customer loyalty, employee efficiency, suggestions for improvements? And what do you punish? Suppliers who consistently are late or make mistakes in materials they deliver to you, employee tardiness or theft, accounts that go beyond thirty days due?

Perhaps you do not think of yourself as having an "incentives system," but the sum total of what you reward and what you punish does indeed make up such a system. It's better to be aware of it.

A wonderful organization development saying goes: "What gets rewarded gets done—and gets done right." That sums up the value of having a good incentives system.

There are both formal and informal incentives. Your formal incentives are items such as salaries, bonuses, awards, public recognition. Informal rewards include such things as attention by the owner, mentoring, expressions of personal appreciation, provision of up-to-date equipment and other resources, and concern for creation or maintenance of a positive working atmosphere.

Similarly, on the side of punishments, some things are public, others are private or confidential.

A person may be denied a raise because of lackluster performance, or perhaps demoted because of inability to match up to the demands of a job description. The ultimate punishment for employees, of course, is firing; however, the mere threat of such, stated or strongly implied, also constitutes a powerful component of your incentives system.

Vis-a-vis suppliers or customers, too, you may levy punishments that are either formal (overt) or informal (less pronounced). A written complaint to a supplier in which you threaten to sever ties if problems persist is an example of a formal punishment. A word of reproach over the telephone without any threat to break off relations is more informal. Filing suit against a customer who is over

120 days late with a major payment certainly constitutes formal punishment. A phone call encouraging the same customer to set up a payment plan with you would be informal.

Know your style. What kind of rewards and punishments have you already been meting out? It's a good idea to write them down and become aware of the kind of system of incentives you have been creating. Then you need to ask: What's been working well for us? What hasn't? Some owners may find they have been too rigid, and need to become more humane. Others may find their system is too slack, and people—from suppliers to customers to employees—have been taking advantage of their easygoing nature.

You will find that what you reward and what you punish has a strong bearing upon the type of culture you have set in place.

Here are some questions that may help you see the picture:

• What do you reward in your business? What do you punish?

• What employee competencies do you value the most?

• Are your rewards and punishments more formal in nature? Or informal?

• Is what you reward in line with your stated objectives?

• What is the ratio of your positive feedback (rewards) to negative feedback (punishments)?

Culture

"Corporate culture defines the rules of the game," says Michael Zwell, Ph.D., in his book *Creating a Culture of Competence.* "It says, 'This is how we do things. This is what we believe. This is how we interact with each other. These are our attitudes toward work.'"

And here's another capsule definition from management consultant Edgar H. Schein: "Culture is the sum total of all the shared, taken-for-granted assumptions that a group has learned throughout its history." That line comes from his work *The Corporate Culture Survival Guide.*

Mostly, culture is shaped in the early days of the business. The culture of a small business is driven by the beliefs, values, and world view of the owner. These are woven into every aspect of the operation. Culture, however, belongs to the group, and thus employees too help to set it in place.

Culture has an intimate relationship to each of the other five areas discussed in this chapter. Each culture determines what technology comes to be engaged. It drives the kind of information that is considered valuable. It is the guiding force behind many of a company's functional departments, systems, and business processes. Each culture will reward and punish a particular array of behaviors. In other words, in one culture you may be rewarded for hard work even though you may work irregular hours of your own choosing; in another culture you may be punished for being even ten minutes late to work, no matter how much good effort you expend on your assigned tasks.

The term "culture" was first used by anthropologists who were studying countries. Culture is what you notice when you travel to a foreign country. Things look different from the way they do at home, and the people behave differently.

Every business has its own particular culture, just as every country does. People will talk about "the IBM way" or "the Microsoft way." Culture is hard to put your finger on, but you can definitely sense it when you step through a company's doors. Much of culture is unspoken, maybe even unconscious, but its presence permeates a company and becomes part of the way employees think and act.

Don't be fooled by simple cultural stereotypes such as "disciplined," "creative," "professional," "empowered," or "open." While these might describe important aspects of a culture, they are too confining. Culture is much more complex and far reaching. It is no easier to decipher a business culture than it is to decipher the culture of another country. Just imagine trying to sum up the culture of the Italians with the word "expressive." It doesn't cover the territory, not at all.

Why spend time, then, trying to decipher a business culture? Because that culture greatly affects a business—yours, a competitor's, a customer's, or that of a supplier upon whom you may depend. As Schein says, "Culture matters."

He goes on to explain: "Culture matters because it is a powerful, latent, and often unconscious set of forces that determine our individual and collective behavior, ways of perceiving, thought patterns, and values. Organizational culture in particular matters because cultural elements determine strategy, goals, and modes of operating. . . .

"It matters because decisions made without awareness of the operative cultural forces may have unanticipated and undesirable consequences. The point is the consequences...could have been predicted, and in some cases they could have been prevented if the culture had been taken seriously in the first place."

You don't simply waltz into a situation and change a whole culture—that of a company any more than you would that of a foreign city. You define what you want to keep, and any aspects you want to change you must begin to pinpoint and work at very carefully. Changing a culture is hard because culture is woven into the fabric of a business. One characteristic of culture is that it is deep and stable. It is supposed to be stable and resistant to change, insofar as one of culture's purposes is to provide a stable and common atmosphere in which a variety of individuals can communicate and operate.

The following questions should help you identify your company culture:

- What are some of the key values of your company?
- What do you notice about the atmosphere of your company that is different from the atmosphere of other companies with which you are familiar?
- What do you see that you especially like and want to keep?
- What do you notice that could stand some improvement?

The Synergy of All Six

As you have been able to appreciate, becoming aware of all six of these areas will be tremendously productive for your business. Beyond that, you will gain greatly if you can see the interrelatedness of technology, information, functions/systems/processes, competencies, incentives, and culture. This may help remove some of the mystery of why things happen in your business the way they do.

Getting all six components to work together in positive synergy is extremely powerful. That is the stuff of great and dynamic organizations.

For additional insights into subjects discussed in this chapter, see *Choice, Change & Organizational Change* by

Clay Carr (American Management Assn., 1996), *Creating a Culture of Competence* by Michael Zwell, Ph.D. (Wiley, 2000), and *The Corporate Cultural Survival Guide* by Edgar H. Schein (Jossey-Bass, 1999).

Excellent firms don't believe in excellence—only in constant improvement and constant change.

— Tom Peters

A man of character finds special attractiveness in difficulty, since it is only by coming to grips with difficulty that he can realize his potentialities.

— Charles De Gaulle

Culture is your number-one priority.

— Herb Kelleher, founder and CEO,
   Southwest Airlines

All great changes are irksome to the human mind, especially those which are attended with great dangers and uncertain effects.

— John Quincy Adams

14

In Business As in Nature— Everything Is Connected

Systems Thinking Gives You an Edge

Everything is connected to everything else.

— Barry Commoner

The first law of ecology, Barry Commoner's line that "everything is connected to everything else," is also a fundamental reality in business—though one that escapes many entrepreneurs.

Many of our popular axioms point up this important reality. We often say, "A chain is only as strong as its weakest link," or "Touch a drum head in one spot, and it resounds all over." In other words, it's a commonplace that all phenomena within a given social body—a family, a company or a town—affect all the other phenomena therein. And yet on an everyday, practical level, we act as if we didn't know or believe that this is really so.

Academic researchers and certain large corporations are coping with such interrelatedness by developing a discipline known as systems engineering. Constantly evolving, system approaches initially concentrated on mechanical systems—the hardware of a corporate setting—and then moved on to categorize "business systems"—management, marketing, accounting. More recently we have had the evolution of "human resource" departments at major companies and an increased focus on the human system and its influence upon corporate evolution.

So we might think of the systems in place at work as three: technical (equipment), operational (processes) and human (people-to-people relations). They can be visualized as three intermeshing gears. If any one system is off-track, obviously it will wreck the intermeshing process and throw the whole business askew.

Does all of this seem too high-flown to be applied to much smaller operations than, say, American Airlines or Xerox? Well, guess again: Systems thinking applies to YOU and your venture, too. In fact, recognizing its worth just might be an important key to your success.

Seeing the Big Picture

Systems thinking views organizations as a whole. It requires a shift in thinking, so that we no longer see each function (production, marketing, sales, accounting, etc.) as separate but rather as parts of one unified operation. We thus see interrelatedness everywhere we look. And we also start to realize that our venture does not exist in isolation but is part of a larger system called "the marketplace."

Peter Senge, in his trail-blazing book *The Fifth Discipline*, suggests that the reason we focus on parts instead of the whole is that, "from a very early age, we are taught to break problems apart, to fragment the world." This tactic, he adds, makes us feel that problem-solving is more manageable. The downside to this, in Senge's explanation, is that "we can no longer see the consequences of our actions; we lose our intrinsic sense of connection to a larger whole." We used to say in American parlance, "Can't see the forest for the trees." A more contemporary expression is "losing sight of the Big Picture."

What may well happen when we lose the Big Picture is that in "solving" a problem with one part of our operation, we may compromise another part.

For instance, let's say you run a three-person graphic arts firm. You haven't given yourself a raise in awhile, and you notice that the competition charges more than you do, so you raise your rates. The rate change "goes down" all right with most of your customers, though you lose a few at the lower end. Suddenly, however, you notice that the customers who have stuck with you are demanding more service and a higher level of quality.

Meanwhile, your two employees, one an accomplished graphic artist and the other a secretary/artist trainee, are complaining of being overworked and suggesting it would be good if you could hire someone part-time or farm out a portion of the work. What have you overlooked here? You forgot to factor into your rate hike a potential customer demand for a higher grade of work, which would then translate into increased pressure on your existing staff.

What you may have done, without realizing it, is move your operation "upmarket." You may in fact have abandoned a market niche that you had comfortably occupied and put yourself in a different niche; now even the competition is different, and so are customer expectations. The new target market might call for a new marketing plan, including new kinds of advertising.

There's nothing wrong with moving up-market as long as you do it consciously. But when you do it haphazardly, without adequate reflection, you could find yourself in turbulent waters and swimming for your life.

Seeing wholes and interrelatedness, however, does not represent the length and breadth of systems thinking. Another important component is seeing changes as a motion picture instead of as snapshots — stepping back and viewing everything as a dynamic process. This is hardest to do when changes are incremental and slow. Even so, you must track such changes if you are going to adjust your business to keep pace.

Many businesses fail because they let gradual change creep up on them and wipe them out. They focus too intently on the day-by-day mini-crises—the new competitor that appears, the employee that announces that she wants to quit, the latest price increase in key supplies. Meanwhile, at a much slower pace, important changes may be building in your market. Missing them or under-rating them could cost you dearly.

The American auto industry provides an example of such myopia. In the early 1960s the Big Three manufacturers dominated the U.S. market. Japanese auto makers had managed only a 4 percent market share. When Japan increased its share to 10 percent in 1967, the Big Three took scant notice. And they didn't adjust their models or marketing enough either when in 1974 the Japanese share had risen to 15 percent. Not until the early 1980s, when the Japanese market share had grown to a hefty 21 percent, did American auto makers react seriously.

The year-by-year changes were not dramatic. Over time, however, they added up to market challenges of the highest importance. This sort of thing can happen in any sector of the economy, including yours.

Feedback in Business Systems

All systems offer us some form of feedback. Feedback

will show us either that changes we are implementing are being accepted and taking hold or that there is a resistance to them that we can ignore only at our peril.

Here's a classic example of feedback everyone can relate to: adjusting the water for your shower. There you are, already under the shower, and it suddenly feels too hot. So what do you do? You turn it down, but by too much! Now the water's too cold. So you jump back, turn down the volume of water and keep adjusting back and forth, more moderately, until you get the water temperature right for you. Now you can take your shower.

Business is very much the same. We swing erratically between doing no advertising at all, for example, and then go to another extreme and spend more than we should on a short campaign. When the campaign brings unsatisfactory results, we shut down our advertising completely again! All the while a more steady, moderately budgeted advertising campaign may have been what was really needed. ("Advertising is not for quitters," is a common axiom in the trade. To be effective, advertising must be steady, consistent, and long term.)

Feedback may not be immediate. And here we have to combat our typical American lack of patience and behave more like the Orientals, who seem to know intuitively that good things, such as success in business, require persistent effort over a long period of time.

The time it may take us to adjust our systems in response to either positive or negative feedback from our market may vary from weeks to months to years. The ideal is to hesitate long enough to verify a trend or a particular kind of customer reaction, but once the evidence is on the table, to move expeditiously to effect the change that we have decided is required.

Smart companies organize feedback. Airlines and motel groups provide short questionnaires for their customers to compliment or criticize accommodations and service. Publications print readership surveys. Good managers spend a lot of time listening to their field reps, not simply telling them what to do. As an entrepreneur, you may not be able to use all the feedback techniques the big boys use, but you can certainly plan to contact your customers to ask them key questions on a regular, planned basis.

So here, to recap briefly, you have a 1-2-3 formula for success:

1. Think in wholes and see interrelatedness among all parts of your operation.

2. See changes as motion pictures, not as snapshots. Be especially watchful for slow, long-term changes in your sector.

3. Pay attention to the feedback that each of your systems will offer you (from colleagues, employees, suppliers, customers, advisors). And go beyond that to organize getting the feedback you need. Then act upon it as soon as you have sifted the evidence and the picture is clear.

FINANCE

BUILD YOUR BUSINESS STRONGER—
AND

15

Educated Guesswork Saves the Day

How to Do a Financial Projection Without Going Totally Bananas

The only thing we have to fear is fear itself.

— Franklin D. Roosevelt

Joe Phillips, a remodeling contractor, has long had a sense that he ought to do some kind of financial projections. However, he simply never knew where to start. Besides, he figured that financial projections were so complex only CPAs and other financial whizzes could handle them.

Nonetheless, the contractor had an inking that if he could do such a projection, it would be very rewarding. In fact, it could even give his business a big lift.

For one thing, this kind of projection is a major component of a classic business plan and an element that banks or other lending agencies will want to inspect carefully before extending you credit. For another, a financial projection becomes a guidepost for your business as you move through the year and access how realistic your judgment of how your company would perform actually was.

If a financial projection of expenses, gross revenues

and net revenues for the forthcoming year would be so valuable, how can Joe Phillips—and you—get started?

Take a Guess

With good guesswork, that's how. That's right: Guesswork.

Since Joe has been in business for three years, he does indeed have some figures with which to work, even if—as is the case in many new businesses—his accounting has thus far been far less than perfect to the decimal point.

Joe should start by developing categories for all expenses, such as rent, equipment amortization, salaries and benefits for himself and employees, insurance, advertising, office supplies, transportation, utilities and so on. Next he should create categories for all revenues, contracting, subcontracting, referral fees and others. He must be careful to separate gross income—the total dollar being paid into his company by his clients—from net income, amount left after all expenses associated with the account have been subtracted.

For each of the three previous years, he should then assign month-by dollar figures to each category of gross income, outgo and—the difference—net (taxable) income.

Now comes the guesswork. Based on what has happened in the past and his vision of how the coming year looks how much income he can reasonably expect and how much he can logically lay out for expenses, our contractor can begin to put down dollar figures in each box for the coming year. He can even do it month by month, measuring in his mind the peaks and valleys of the construction business.

So can you, though your business may be as far afield from construction as freelance marketing, import/export or janitorial services. Like Joe Phillips, you can come to see—I hope through the chapter you are now in the midst of reading—that doing a financial projection for your business is an achievable goal.

If you are in your very first year of business, the guesswork about revenue will have to be even more hypothetical than in Joe's projection. But guess you must. It's the only way to put numbers in all the boxes you have created. In other words, don't let fear about "getting it right" stand in the way of doing it at all. Otherwise, you'll freeze, and no finished projection will ever emerge from your rummaging through your records and making several false starts.

As we'll see in a minute, those guesses will later have to be refined through a process of consultation with others, such as an accountant, a banker, and possibly someone else who understands your field of business well.

Refining the Numbers

Let's return to Joe Phillips' case. After Joe has put down his best guesses for each category, month by month, for the coming year, he should put his draft projections aside for at least a few days. Coming back to the figures with a fresh eye, the contractor should rethink his guesses, category by category. What variations might he have left out of his calculations? Do the industry journals forecast a good, bad or average year for remodeling? What discretionary income are consumers likely to have in the coming year? What's the inflation index like for equipment Joe might have to purchase? For insurance rates? For other likely expenditures? Can he raise his prices at all? Increase the volume of work his firm can bid on?

Rethinking Assumptions

A few quick calls to his suppliers, his advertising outlets (Yellow Pages and others), insurance agency, utilities, and so on will help him rethink his assumptions and give a better "edge" to his projections. Conversations with others in his field or in tangential fields (such as building supply store managers) will sharpen his perception of the public's buying mood and spending power.

Armed with better information, Joe can return to his plans and tighten up his figures.

After one or two rewrites of his financial projections, Joe is ready to take his estimates to others for review. Family and friends are a good place to start. Even though they have the least expertise, they often come up with items that we have overlooked, or they have enough familiarity with what we do to question our judgment on this or that item.

Joe Phillips—or you—may be lucky and have an uncle, aunt or cousin who is an accountant. In this case, getting a friendly review may cost no more than a lunch check. If not, Joe (and you) should not hesitate to spend a little money to have a financial professional review the draft projection. (If your budget is very tight, try a banker with whom you have developed a good rapport. He or she may do this for you as a free service. So will Service Corps of Retired Executives (SCORE) volunteers who have an accounting background.)

Small business counselors at many community colleges and local Small Business Development Centers offer free counseling and welcome you to take advantage of their time and talents. In some cases, they can help you refine your projections by checking them against a software package.

Such centers, along with the many SCORE offices throughout the country, can be found in the Yellow Pages and also in the calendar section of business journals.

After Joe comes back from a series of reviews of his figures—with an accountant, a banker and a small business counselor—he is quite amazed at how professional and how convincing his final projection has become. He decides that he now agrees with F.D.R.'s celebrated remark, "The only thing we have to fear is fear itself."

So put aside your fears and start on your own financial projections—now.

I don't know any CEO who doesn't love numbers.

— Jeffery Silverman, CEO, PlyGem Industries Ltd.

Businesses always have problems. Numbers tell you where the problems are and how worried you should be.

— Jack Stack, CEO, Springfield Remanufacturing Corporation, and author, **The Great Game of Business**

Take time to deliberate, but when the time for action has arrived, stop thinking and go in.

— Napoleon Bonaparte

Our doubts are traiters, and make us lose the good we oft might win by fearing to attempt.

— William Shakespeare

Celebrate your success and find humor in your failures. Don't take yourself so seriously. Loosen up and everyone around you will loosen up. Have some fun and always show enthusiasm. When all else fails put on a costume and sing a silly song.

— Sam Walton

The significant problems we face today cannot be solved at the same level of thinking we were at when we created them.

— Albert Einstein

We cannot become what we want to be by remaining what we are.

— Max DePree, author, **The Art of Leadership,** and former CEO, Herman Miller, Inc.

16

The Banker Is Not Your Enemy

Study the Way Bankers Think— Before You Ask for a Loan

A big disappointment in life is the discovery that the man who writes the finance company ads isn't the one who makes the loans.

— The London Free Press

The business loan can inject life into new ventures and light a fire under older ones. But getting the loan when it's needed can be tricky. To find out what bankers want to know when they're faced with a loan application, from a banker like yours, I interviewed Thomas R., a vice president at a suburban bank. Here's what he had to say.

RG: Tom, we've both had careers that have put us in touch with examining people as financial risks, you with a bank and I as a financial consultant. What would you say about the differences between dreaming and reality for entrepreneurs. . . ?

TR: In small business classes, as you surely know since you teach some of these, people have all these great ideas. They just know it's going to work—their pet store idea or an invention of theirs or their very competitive maid service or whatever. It's what they haven't thought of yet, or what they don't know, that a banker has to worry about.

The Big Four

RG: There are basically four criteria that every loan officer has to look at when examining a business plan or interviewing a prospect, aren't there? Experience has taught me to look at the applicant's available investment capital, his or her capacity to actually carry out the plan and generate the cash flow to pay back the debt. Then the other two key factors that seem to enter in are collateral and credit worthiness.

TR: Those are the big four, yes.

RG: Well, what's your priority among these four?

TR: It's always a give and take. In most cases, however, I'd put either capital or capacity to make a go of the business in the first place. However, you can always offset weak points by being stronger in other areas. Tradeoffs. For example, a poor credit history can be counterbalanced by excellent cash flow or high capitalization or possibly even by a partnering arrangement with someone who is a proven success.

RG: I notice you emphasized capitalization again. So, if someone puts enough money into a project, that person's chances for qualifying for a loan increase dramatically. On the other hand, if the applicant cannot demonstrate through a carefully thought-out projection of cash flow that money for repayment will be available, no bank is gong to advance the funds.

Don't most banks look for the validity of assumptions that underlie a cash-flow projection, such as the reasonability of growth projections, of estimated expenses, and so on?

TR: Absolutely. Banking is a risk business. But all banks try to minimize the risks as much as possible. We're going to look at the degree of reliability of a business plan overall, and specifically any cash-flow projections. Bankers think with a lot of "what ifs."

Spell Out the Risks

We want to see the risks spelled out. For instance, can this person, who may have been a salaried employee up until now, really learn how to be a disciplined self-starter? What happens if the product or service is not well accepted at first? Or if strong competition gets the idea and moves into your market? Or if your startup costs go way past your initial projections? Might technology just on the horizon tender your product obsolete?

Or take an example of a seasonal business, such as renting mountain bikes or rafting equipment. A business like this may go great guns for four or five months. But have the principals adequately planned for covering all their salary and rent and other ongoing expenses for the rest of the year? If they haven't, even a successful seasonal run may not be enough to cover their monthly loan payments.

RG: As a consultant, I try to find ways to help people in the struggle to achieve a healthy balance between enthusiastic and optimistic while not ducking the necessary reality checks on the "what ifs."

Let's take a hypothetical example of a man who has been working for an engineering firm. Now he wants to branch out on his own. He is going to need an office, a small staff, and equipment. Furthermore, let's say he already has a number of clients lined up.

TR: And he's able to prove that?

RG: Yes. Signed contracts and all. So he has a track record and he has clients waiting for him to do their projects. Now he needs a $200,000 startup loan. What else are you going to be looking for in his business plan?

TR: What comes to my mind immediately are the negative possibilities: What is his reason for leaving his job and trying to start his own company? Was he a good employee?

In good with his firm? What makes him think he'll be a good business owner? Just being a good engineer is not enough. He may have made a wonderful line person, but he might be a lousy boss. How can he assure us he's going to be success at hiring and managing others?

Then how detailed is his business plan? How many hurdles can he see down the road, and what is his proactive approach to anticipating them and overcoming them?

Write a Detailed Business Plan

RG: There's something about the process of doing a detailed business plan, isn't there? In the course of that, you simply are forced to examine all the key aspects of your business. And that's very eye-opening. Doing a business plan teaches you so much of all the contingencies you have to allow for... Every time you do a business plan you get better at it. I think the process just makes you a better business person.

TR: Business plans can be done in all sorts of ways. Do-it-yourself kits, community college entrepreneurial development offices, and through CPAs and other consultants. Sometimes paying somebody $2,000-$3,000 to help you develop a professional plan that targets SBA or other financing can be worth it. It's a great idea to get help if you can spare the money to do it. Otherwise, there are fairly good books and software packages or free advice services, such as SCORE or Small Business Development Centers and other community college centers, that can improve your plan substantially.

RG: Can we talk a bit about collateral? How important is it? What sort of things are considered good collateral?

TR: Collateral is important, but keep in mind that the bank really does not want to own your house, your two cars and your pedigreed cocker spaniel. I've got people who come into the bank and say, "Take the house, take the car, take the machinery—just give me a loan." But we're not in the liquidation or resale business. What we want is money in and money out.

RG: Also, it takes a certain heartlessness to be foreclosing on people's homes and taking their possessions. Financial officers don't really like to do that, do they? And then you have to get attorneys involved, and it gets messy.

Getting back to capital for a moment, shouldn't applicants raise capital from family and friends before they go to see a banker?

TR: Yes, definitely. The more money you can come up with before you ask for a loan, the more chance there is that you will get your loan. The best time to borrow money is when you don't have a desperate need for it.

Finding the Right Bank

Let me bring up another point here. Not all banks do all kinds of loans as well as other banks may. Banks often acquire expertise in certain industrial sectors such as, perhaps, restaurants or construction companies or inventions. You should do some research on which banks have done which kinds of loans the most. If you want money to start a deli, why go to some bank that almost never puts out money for restaurants? See a bank that knows the lunch business.

RG: Tom, as a banker, you probably run into people who think of you as just a naysayer or someone throwing a wet blanket over their ideas. How do you respond to that?

TR: It's sometimes hard for an entrepreneur to appreciate the banker's perspective. The entrepreneur is usually focused on his or her vision and the direction in which they're headed. They'll tend to think, "people who give me negative feedback are not in camp. They're the enemy." But really, we're not. Playing the devil's advocate, so to speak, is a way of being helpful. My role is to get people to go back to the drawing board when they have to, or chart out their course much more carefully. What a banker is really trying to do is to help you prevent those huge, costly mistakes that can ruin your business. Try viewing the banker as an ally, even when he or she may be saying, "Your plan isn't good enough yet." Go back and make your plan good enough. Then you'll get your loan.

———————————

[A sound accounting system] not only reveals our mistakes— it shows us what a good job we're doing.

> — Bror R. Carlson, Director of Accounting, International Minerals & Chemical Co.

One of the chief sources of success in manufacturing is the introduction and strict maintenance of a perfect system of accounting so that responsibility for money and materials can be brought home to every man.

> — Andrew Carnegie, founder, U.S. Steel

The secret of business is to know something that nobody else knows.

> — Aristotle Onassis

CHAPTER

17

Getting the Money You Need

Turn a Good Loan Proposal into a Great One

Entrepreneurs are simply those who understand that there is little difference between obstacle and opportunity and are able to turn both to their advantage.

— Victor Kiam, CEO, Remington Products

At some point in the life of nearly every business, there will come a need to seek financing from an outside source, usually a bank or savings and loan. Many small business owners enter into this process with fear and trembling. And indeed some of the fear is justified, for compiling the right data and making the right case with a bank is a complex challenge.

While no one can promise you that if you simply follow steps one through nine as outlined in this or that book, your loan application will be a shoo-in, there are indeed very specific steps you can take to greatly improve your chances of the banker's saying "yes." Here are five.

Do Your Homework

When you are developing a business, an ability to do good research and use it confers a tremendous competitive advantage. "Re-search" means simply to "search again." In regard to fine-tuning your business plan, searching again could spell the difference between your venture's getting a "yes" from a banker and being properly financed— or a discouraging "no" that leaves you twisting in the wind.

Spend plenty of time researching your industry, market, customers, and competition. While most of you have done such study to one degree or another, I am suggesting that you go even deeper. You want to end up with twice as much information as you think you need for your plan. You don't have to put everything but the kitchen sink into it. But you do want to have additional information in your head so that when the banker poses questions you may not have dealt with on paper, you will nevertheless have answers. Nothing impresses bankers more than your having good, solid answers to their questions.

Naturally, you also want to anticipate many typical bank questions by addressing such matters in your business plan. There are many good books that will take you through all the sections of a business plan and help you frame your own material as data.

The areas you want to address in your plan—in addition to information about your own specific product or products: your personal, career, and financial preparation; and your management team—include

- Industry information
- Target marketing data (statistics and trends)
- Competition
- Customer profile (who your customers are, how numerous they are, where they live, what they want, and what they will buy).

This last item, by the way, how customers choose whom they will do business with, is particularly important, and it is often overlooked in business plans.

The last reason to spend extra time doing research is that—as you will find to your considerable delight—it will make you an expert in your field, whether that field is running a cappucino bar or selling printing contracts. You want potential customers to recognize your competence and knowledgeability. This will give you a decisive edge when you are operating your business. People who are looking for a particular product or service are drawn to someone who is very knowledgeable.

Research approaches will vary from one field to another. Your local chamber of commerce, Small Business Development Center, SCORE office, or university, college, or community college will get you off to a good start. Some public libraries are especially good at helping with business research. Then, too, each field normally has its trade journals and annual industry association reports. Don't shortchange doing your own "walking around research," either. Check the Yellow Pages and talk to people in your own marketing area. If a field is not too crowded, you may find that you can even approach competitors candidly, and often they will actually help you flesh out your profile of the industry.

List the Assumptions Behind Your Projections

Every business plan is built upon assumptions, such as percentages of anticipated growth; how much needed equipment will cost and when you will purchase it; sales and marketing expectations, such as response rates to direct mail advertising; when you will need additional space and how much you will pay to rent or buy it; when you will need staff and how the staff will be paid.

In many business plans, assumptions are more or less

woven in but are often not spelled out very clearly. This is a mistake. Actually listing your assumptions in crystal-clear language gives you two added benefits:

• It shows the banker that you yourself have a lucid idea of what the underlying assumptions are.

• It forces you to consciously review these assumptions and question them hard yourself (before you have to face the banker, who will question them even harder).

Listing assumptions gives you the chance to ask yourself, "Is this really reasonable?" Value the process—don't rush it. The process itself can teach you much about what it will take for you to succeed.

The way to check your assumptions is to take a calculator to all the figures in your plan. Start by analyzing every increase in costs or sales or profits or whatever you have put down. Most of your assumptions will take the form of percents of increase from one quarter (or year) to the next. Calculate all of those percentages. Use this formula: New period minus old period. Divide the result by the old period and multiply by 100 to get your percent of increase. If, for example, your sales begin at $58,000 and increase to $66,120, your calculations would go like this: 66,120 – 58,000 = 8,120. Divide 8,120 by 58,000 to get 0.14. Multiply 0.14 by 100, and your result is a 14 percent increase in sales.

Look for reasons behind those increases. Ask yourself, "What would cause my sales to go up by 28 percent?" Try to see how sales increases relate to marketing, staffing, and equipment purchases. Determine which of these usually happens first and which are consequences.

Include separate pages in your business plan to detail the following:

1. The way money from a loan will be used, including

how much will cover startup or expansion costs and what will cover working capital over a period of time.

2. Staff needed for startup or expansion, salaries to be paid, and when you plan to hire staff.

3. Equipment needed during the period, what it will cost, when you will buy it, and how you will amortize it.

Define Risks and Ways to Mitigate Them

Every venture has its risks. That is the nature of being in business. You will improve the business plan if you actually list the risks you will be courting. What, in other words, could go wrong? What problems have similar businesses had? What are the special risks in the project that you are proposing to establish and develop?

Once again, listing these risks will force you to rethink your plan. It also makes the risks a little more real. Both of these things are good for you. Aim for balance, however. Both extremes are to be avoided; you want neither to ignore the risks you'll be facing nor to focus on them so hard they end up scaring the wits out of you.

The most common risk is slow growth or market acceptance. You plan on your business growing at a rate of 10 to 15 percent a year. Well, what will happen if it grows at only 7 to 9 percent a year? That is a real risk, especially when you have staffed up or invested in equipment for a higher rate of growth.

Factors that might mitigate the risks in a case of slower-than-expected growth are flexibility to reduce staff, for example, or potential for developing other products.

Here are some other risks you might consider (and the list is far from exhaustive): Management underestimation of major problem (such as equipment breakdown), poor implementation of the business plan, difficulty in getting needed staff, aggressive response from a competitor, possible government regulation changes, rapid changes in market forces, a nuisance suit from a customer.

Try to list at least three risks that you and your business face. Listing five is not too many. Then provide your response to each risk. Show your banker that you are going into the fray with your eyes wide open, and you are ready to maneuver around obstacles as they may present themselves.

Provide Both Optimal and Worst-Case Projections

All bankers expect a business plan to contain a set of financial projections, mostly tied to the venture's future pattern of success. What really impresses a banker, however, is seeing a second set of projections linked to a worst-case scenario. These projections take off from the same present-time data as the more optimistic projections, but they demonstrate what will happen if everything does not go as the entrepreneur hopes. Often the worst-case scenario may end up being closer to reality than the optimal projection.

Your worst-case projection must show how you will keep up your loan payments even if your expansion is not on schedule or if unexpected expenses occur. The banker knows that these scenarios are possible, and he or she will normally be impressed when you demonstrate that you know too, as well as by the fact that you have budgeted to account for sub-par growth.

Doing worst-case projections causes you to rethink your business plan. This stepping back from the plan and going over everything with a fine-tooth comb is an invaluable process and a good counter-force to the typical entrepreneurial enthusiasm that wants to view the world through rose-colored glasses. Remember, though: Your worst-case projections of slower growth and higher expenses or tepid market acceptance of your product must still show enough cash flow for you to keep pace with your loan payment schedule. It will obviously do you no good if your worst-case scenario cannot cover your debt.

Have Others Review Your Plan

Entrepreneurs have gained a reputation for being Lone Rangers. This stereotype may have rung true in the past, but it is less accurate today. Small business owners do not operate in a vacuum. They need the support of other people. This is especially true when you are doing a business plan. As Proverbs says, "There is wisdom in many counselors." Seek competent help.

A well-rounded business plan is usually the result of blending a number of different perspectives. Hence the wisdom of showing your own well-thought-out draft of a plan to such people as small business development advisors, an accountant, a lawyer, a marketing consultant, and others who have won their spurs in business. Each of these individuals will have a sharply nuanced perspective, and all these perspectives are valid and useful. By taking into account the advice of others, you will build into your plan a maturity and sophistication that bankers and potential investors will appreciate.

Having others review your plan will also alert you to risks you may not have considered and probably will also lead to suggestions for heading off or mitigating those risks, too.

––––––––––––

The victors of the battles of tomorrow will be those who can best harness thought to action.

— B.C. Forbes, founder, **Forbes** magazine

I want something not just to invest in. I want something to believe in.

— Anita Roddick, founder, The Body Shop

Kites rise the highest against the wind—not with it.

— Winston Churchill

There is no security on earth, there is only opportunity.

— General Douglas MacArthur

Success seems to be connected with action. Successful men keep moving. They make mistakes, but they don't quit.

— Conrad Hilton, founder, Hilton Hotels

Staying in the Black

Cash Flow—The Monitor of Your Business' Health

The only irreparable mistake in business is to run out of cash. . . when you run out of cash, they take you out of the game.

— Harold Geneen, former CEO of IT&T

Cash flow is a term that is much heard but not always well understood. Just what is cash flow, anyway? And why is it so important?

First, it isn't called cash flow for nothing. Cash flows through a business just as blood flows through your body. And it is every bit as vital.

Cash flow for a business is similar to a personal checking account for an individual or family. You have cash coming in—either paper money or checks or credit card charges—and later (much later, you hope) cash going out, in any of the same forms.

A sale is not counted until the cash actually hits the register or your checking account. And a bill is just an annoying piece of paper until you put a check with it and kiss the money good-bye.

As with many aspects of life, cash flow has its upside and its downside. Happiness is when your cash flow is positive—you have more money coming in than you need to ship out. In periods when this is true, you can tell the bank (and the bank really does want to know), "My cash flow is positive right now."

Negative cash flow is a short-term bother. In the longer term a consistent pattern of negative cash flow will kill your business. Even though your business overall may be profitable, if you keep running short of cash and can't satisfy your creditors on a timely basis, they may be tolerant for awhile—but not forever. When they lose patience, you may have to miss a payroll or roll over your bank loan. Before you can say J. Paul Getty, you're in bankruptcy court!

What's the difference between a cash flow statement and an income or profit-and-loss (P/L) statement? Income statements record a sale when the promise to buy is made, whereas a cash flow statement tracks the actual transfer of money, incoming and outgoing. A cash flow statement has mainly to do with when you get the money or pay it out.

Why Is Cash Flow So Crucial?

Day by day, hardened business owners—the ones who have survived it all—think in cash flow and are apt to proclaim, "Positive cash flow is even more important than your mother."

Cash on hand is one important measure of your business' economic health. The more resources you have, the more options you have: to upgrade your equipment, to launch a new product, to hire another person, to pursue a new market, to spend more on advertising, and so on.

Some business experts say that inadequate cash flow is the major reason for business failure. And poor cash management may sink even the most promising business, no matter how alert and hard-working its staff may be.

Banks put more emphasis on your cash flow statements than on your P/L statements. One reason is that when your monthly loan payments come due, the money has to come from cash flow. The first thing a banker will ask you about is cash flow. Responding with a blank stare when you are asked about your cash flow will NOT help you get a loan.

The bank will ask to see historical and projected cash flow statements to qualify you for a business loan. This is frequently the trickiest part of a business plan. If you haven't got your business into operation yet, you can do only a projected statement.

How will you know when money will come in or go out? You usually must rely on well-thought-out assumptions. These assumptions are critical. If they don't stand up to the bank's logic, forget about your loan. You won't get it.

Monitoring Cash Flow

Before you can improve your cash flow, you have to be aware of where you are with it, and that means you must track your cash flow carefully and well. This can seem like a huge pain, because you really want to do whatever it is you do well and not hassle too much with accounting. But the point of this chapter is to help take some of the pain out of the process, so hang in there.

In its simplest form, monitoring cash flow means only recording the money that comes in and the money that goes out. Everything else is just an expansion of that exercise. The encouraging thing is that almost everybody is doing this in one form or another, if only through notations in a checkbook or through the mechanical processes of a cash register.

By expansion I mean adding detail to your recordings.

For example, a store might keep track of cash flow product line by product line. A service business might do it by region or by market. Frequently, however, such tracking has a lot to do with trying to determine which lines are more profitable and which ones are less. Some lines might have a much better cash flow than others because customers pay immediately.

Generating a do-it-yourself cash flow statement calls on only elementary math. You start with cash coming in— cash sales and receivables as they are paid. The total of these two items gives you what's known as "cash in." You get your total "cash out" by adding up salaries, rent, telephone, utilities, supplies, marketing expenses, and so on as they are paid.

Your net cash flow for any given period is the difference between your total cash in and your total cash out. This is the figure you want to keep positive. Stay in the black, stay out of the red—that's pretty much the name of the game.

From one month to another the rise or fall of your cash balances will give you (and your bank) the trends for your business. Frequently cash flow statement will finish with a summary of main indicators: balance at the beginning of the month, net cash flow during the month, and the closing balance at the month's end.

Having cash available and accessible is called "liquidity" and is highly desirable. Ideally, a business should aim to have twice as much cash and current assets (accounts receivable and inventory) as the total of bills due within the year. The difference between these liquid assets and total bills is called "working capital." For those of you who prefer not to live on the edge, this working capital is your safety net.

Generating Cash

Day by day you will want to generate as much cash as possible. What are the ways you can do this?

There are seven ways to increase your cash:

- by making cash sales,
- by reducing costs,
- by converting accounts receivable into cash,
- by converting your inventory into cash,
- by collecting interest income,
- by borrowing moncy (increasing debt), and
- by issuing stock.

The most common and obvious ways of increasing cash are the first two. They account for perhaps 80% of your cash increases. "Converting accounts receivable into cash" usually means changing your credit policy so that people have to pay you sooner or making your collections of slow payers more aggressive. The other ways of raising cash are self-explanatory.

Improving Your Business Decisions

When your awareness of cash flow is low, you really are not mentally set to make good business decisions. You are leaving out a critical element. It follows that the more you improve your awareness of your cash flow, and the more closely you monitor it, the more able you will become to make the right decisions.

Make it a habit to track cash flow as a regular practice every day, at the end of every week, then every month, every quarter and every year. This is the kind of discipline that every entrepreneur really needs if he or she hopes to make it for the long haul. After all, if you believe in your product or service, you want others to believe in its value too so that you can be successful. And if what you have to sell is worthwhile, don't sabotage your own success potential by neglecting or mismanaging your cash.

———————

Happiness is positive cash flow.

— Anonymous

A state of statistical control in not a natural state for a process; it is an achievement.

— W. Edwards Deming

The ancestor of every action is a thought.

— Ralph Waldo Emerson

You must constantly guard against the trap of falling into a routine of remaining busy with unimportant chores that will provide you with an excuse to avoid meaningful challenge or opportunities that could change your life for the better.

— Og Mandino, inspirational speaker and author of **The Greatest Salesman in the World**

Section VI

MARKETING

BUILD YOUR BUSINESS STRONGER—
AND DO

Three Ways to Increase Revenues— and How to Combine All Three

Drive thy business, or it will drive thee.

— Benjamin Franklin

What if I were to ask you, "What is the best way to increase your sales?" If you're like most business people, you'd answer, "Simple. Find more customers." While this is certainly the most common way to grow a business, it also happens to be the most time consuming. And the most costly.

It is indeed one of the three ways to increase business revenues. The other two ways are easier, however, and cost less. They are: 1) to increase the average sales amount per transaction, and 2) to increase frequency of purchase. Both these ways leverage your current customers.

Now the best way of all to grow your business is to combine all three ways. That is, you add new customers, you increase the average amount of sale, and you increase purchase frequency. If you do all three things at once, you will maximize your business growth.

Aim for increasing revenues by 10 percent through each way. Ten plus ten plus ten will give you an impressive 30 percent growth!

Adding 10 percent more customers, for example, is probably quite do-able. If you are a marketing consultant with ten current clients, just one more will achieve your goal of a 10 percent increase. If you have a breakfast and lunch place that grosses $1,000 a day, just another $100 per day from new customers will do the trick.

To take a closer look at how you can add customers, increase sale amounts, and increase frequency, let's follow the scenario of a young sports massage therapist whom we'll call "Ericka."

Having been a licensed massage therapist for one year, Ericka now wants to maximize her business growth. She decides to start by attracting new customers.

Through a business coach, Ericka learns that there are three parts to the process of integrating new customers into her business:

- generating leads or prospects
- "converting" the prospects into paying customers
- retaining those new customers and making them into "regulars."

Ericka takes her coach's advice and begins to think through what she wants to communicate to her prospects. She works on hammering out her "Unique Selling Proposition." This USP explains what a particular business does that is unique and how that uniqueness benefits customers or clients—gives them the best deal for their dollars. It also, therefore, answers the key question, "What's in it for me?" (WIIFM).

An avid athlete herself—she lettered in tennis in high school and college—Ericka has a strong personal background in sports combined with comprehensive training in massage. She works on athletes day in and day out, so she is experienced with the types of injuries and pain that athletes can suffer. She also works hard at being the best sports massage therapist in town.

She has become quite good at helping athletes heal rapidly from their bumps, bruises, twists, and sprains, and return to their best form. This expertise in rapid healing and optimum performance is Ericka's USP.

Now Ericka is ready to generate some leads. She brainstorms ways to find potential customers and comes up with the following ideas. She will volunteer at local races. Do free massages once a month at a local running equipment store. Design a structured referral program with current clients. Do joint promotions with local sporting goods stores. Have an Open House. Put a simple ad in the local sports enthusiasts magazine. Join a running club to network. Join a leads group. Network with local sports doctors. Hand out her business card wherever she goes.

The important thing when brainstorming is just to write down every idea that comes to mind. Do not edit or limit. Now is the time to get five to ten ideas down on paper. Later, you can go back and highlight the best three or four that you want to pursue.

Ericka decides to pursue working on a referral program, volunteering at local races, networking with local sports doctors, and handing out business cards wherever she goes. She might come back and implement some of her other ideas later. Marketing, she knows, is a matter of trial and error. When something works, do more of that!

Improve Your Sales Conversion Rate

To encourage prospects to try out her service, she

offers a discount for the first massage (50 percent off). This is to reduce the resistance to buying something that customers are not sure will be valuable to them. This is called risk reversal, or reducing the buying barrier.

Ericka can do this because she knows that a new customer will usually see her once a week or every other week for about one to two months. About one half of her customers will see her, she knows from past experience, on a somewhat regular basis. You too can offer discounts, just like Ericka did, when you know that you will make most of your money on repeat sales.

Ericka decides to do two other things to improve her selling or conversion rate. For one, she offers an unconditional guarantee. Not a weak-worded "100 percent guaranteed," but something like, "If this massage does not noticeably improve your healing and increase your performance, I will insist that you take your money back."

Sounds pretty bold, doesn't it? Well, Ericka is confident that her work does improve healing and does increase performance. What she says isn't "hype." And she is willing to give a small percentage of clients their money back (5-10 percent) in exchange for the considerable increase in people willing to try her services than otherwise might without the bolder guarantee.

The other thing that Ericka does to help make sales is she regularly asks her most satisfied customers for letters of recommendation, or testimonials. Since she tries to give the best quality massage her customers have ever experienced, many of her clients even offer to write a testimonial letter for her. And she is building a book of these letters to increase her own confidence and to have letters to show to prospective clients. It is great when she can show a prospective client suffering from tennis elbow a letter from a previous client who had great results on their tennis elbow.

With Ericka's specialty, expertise, and level of service, she has no trouble keeping clients satisfied and having people continue to see her. One thing that helps is that she stays in touch with people; she follows up to check on how they are doing by phone or, if they prefer, by e-mail. This kind of communication and follow-up really helps build long-term relationships.

Another thing you should strive to deliver is better than expected service. Exceed, that is, your clients' expectations. This involves your knowing just what they do expect, then providing even more. It doesn't take huge increases in service. Ericka, for instance, does this by explaining more about the client's injury, pointing out the affected muscles on her wall chart and by offering simple tips that the client can follow at home to speed recovery— handouts on exercises, dieting, and vitamin therapy, for example.

Increase Average Purchase Amount

Ericka's average client spends the usual $60 for a one-hour massage. A good start. However, Ericka knows that she can improve that number.

When was the last time you were in a McDonalds? Didn't a counter person ask if you wanted to "add on" a food item—such as a salad or a dessert? This is the most common way to increase average purchase amount. Other methods include the bump (having someone buy a larger amount, such as a 1 1/2-hour massage instead of the usual one-hour), point of purchase advertising (signs to induce extra buying), and cross selling (selling related products and services, such as a home-massage book or massage creams, etc.).

There should be nothing blatant, or "pushy," about

these methods. Each item must add genuine value for the client. For instance, a longer massage provides more time for healing work. All the usual benefits of massage are increased, including better blood flow to affected areas, releasing the trauma that can be stored in a muscle from an injury, and deeply relaxing the injured muscles and surrounding tissue. Also the extended massage allows the therapist more time to gently warm up the muscles before she does deeper body work. This in turn provides for more therapeutic and healing work than a massage where the muscles have not been warmed up as much.

Ericka also decides to offer gift certificates. Very satisfied customers will naturally want to share the experience of massage with someone they know and care about. The certificates offer the perfect way to introduce someone to massage, all the while communicating that you appreciate that family member or friend.

Increase Purchase Frequency

The last of the three methods is to get your regular clientele to patronize your business more often. Think "Frequent Flyer miles." In other words, the way to get people to use your services more frequently is to reward them for doing so.

The first promotion Ericka develops is one that says "If you come and receive seven massages, you will get the eighth one for free." This "carrot on a stick" encourages her clients to step up their regularity with her. Those, for instance, who may have been getting a massage only four or five times a year may well increase to seven in order to get the bonus massage. The once-a-month crowd may be tempted to move their schedule to once every two weeks. And so forth.

Ericka realizes, of course, that this "deal" effectively reduces her hourly rate from $60 an hour to $52.50 an hour. The increase in business, however, more than makes up for the $7.50 "loss."

Another idea Ericka has is to offer a special whereby people can purchase an eight-massage package in advance for the price of seven sessions. The reward for frequency is the same. This way, however, allows Ericka to receive all the money in advance. That is wonderful for cash flow.

Her last notion is to offer special events during the typically "slow" times of the year. Thus she has certain two-week periods during which all massages are 25% off. This kind of business insures that she has plenty of cash on hand for rent, utilities and other fixed items, no matter what.

Specials also give Ericka a chance to telephone or otherwise contact all her clients, including those she hasn't heard from in awhile, to let them know how they can enjoy a massage at a discount rate.

Finally, Ericka can also tell her clients that the discounts are her way of saying "Thank you" for all the business they have given her in the past. This one wins for everyone.

Combine All Three Methods

While each of the methods described above will help expand a business, the most powerful thing you can do is to work all three together to generate a multiplicity of results. Or even exponential results. You build momentum when you combine the methods and do several different kinds of promotion all at once. You can also maximize your business growth.

To wrap up here, remember that effective marketing starts with a mindset. The mindset should say, "There's always one or more ways to increase sales. My only job is to discover those ways, and put them into practice."

The master of marketing mindsets and methods is Jay Abraham. I cannot recommend too highly his book, *Getting Everything You Can Out of All You've Got* (Truman Talley Books/St. Martin's Press, 2000). It should be required reading for anyone interested in maximizing his or her business growth.

———————

People are always blaming their circumstances for what they are. I don't believe in circumstances. The people who get on in this world are the people who get up and look for the circumstances they want, and, if they can't find them, make them.

— George Bernard Shaw

Business has only two functions—marketing and innovation.

— Peter Drucker

Marketing is far too important to leave to the marketing department.

— David Packard, cofounder, Hewlett-Packard

CHAPTER 20

You and Your Business Are Unique

There's Only One Business in the World Like Yours—Capitalize on It!

Always bear in mind that your own resolution to success
is far more important than any other one thing.

— Abraham Lincoln

A quick quiz: Name these companies by their slogans:
1. "When it absolutely, positively has to be there overnight."
2. "When you're Number Two, you have to try harder."
3. "Fresh, hot pizza delivered to your door in 30 minutes or less—or it's free."

These slogans aim to crystallize in the mind of the consumer just how each company serves its public like nobody else.

This uniqueness is commonly called a "unique selling proposition," or USP.

And it is one of the most powerful marketing tools anyone has ever dreamed of.

Many now-gigantic businesses can trace their point of exploding into growth from the date when they launched their USP onto the marketplace, like the three whose slogans are quoted above. (I'll bet you guessed them all—

Number 1 is Federal Express, Number 2 is Avis, and Number 3 is Domino's Pizza.)

Each company has gone to great lengths to stand out from its competition, each has captured that uniqueness in a memorable slogan, and each has become a powerhouse in the American business community.

Perhaps you do not aspire to build your venture into an Avis or a Federal Express, but you probably hope to be bigger and more secure than you are now. Brainstorming your way to your USP can make a difference.

What's Special about You?

Start with the premise that you are indeed unique—and so is your coffee shop or your direct marketing service or your public relations agency. After all, being unique is just what we are as human beings. No two of us are alike. Similarly, no two businesses are exactly alike either.

Next, list your own special qualities. What special training or experience do you have? What stands out about your products or services? What do you consider your strengths? Write all these things down.

Continuing the process, ask yourself: How do I serve my customers like nobody else? What would they say about me and my company that potential customers or clients would understand as complimentary?

It won't take long before, Bingo!, something jumps out at you, something you can put your finger on and claim as your own personal USP. Perhaps you can identify yourself as an editorial consultant who will never say die—always ready to revise, revise and revise until the text acquires just the right flavor or tone. Maybe you are the pet groomer who goes the extra mile with each dog or cat or parrot, so that the animal goes home with a glow. Or could it be that your bookstore has a combination of published products difficult to match anywhere else, such as the History & Mystery Bookstore in Oak Park, Illinois?

Get the Word Out

Whatever you come up with, the next challenge is to highlight just that quality in your promotional materials. It won't help much if only you know and understand your USP. The clients or customers have to know. Conrad Berke, author of *Entrepreneur* magazine's book *Successful Advertising for Small Businesses*, tells his readers: "You need to show how you can make a valuable difference in your customers' lives." And Sarah White and John Woods, authors of *Do-It-Yourself Advertising*, say that dramatic power in advertising comes from positioning your company and your products "as clearly distinct from your competition."

Here the trick is to be as specific as possible. It's not enough to claim that your product is better than the competition or that you offer the best value in a certain market. Customers have heard all that before. They are waiting for YOU to spell out your distinctiveness much more concretely.

A key step at this stage is to back away from your perspective on your product or service. Try trading places with a client or customer and see what that person sees when he or she exchanges hard-earned cash for whatever it is you have to offer. Consciously or unconsciously, customers are always asking themselves, "What's in it for me?" (WIIFM, in marketing jargon.)

Remember, the customer buys from you because he or she is getting more than could be obtained elsewhere —whether in quantity, quality, or value. Jay Abraham, a highly paid marketing consultant ($3,000 an hour), says succinctly: "You have to give people a compelling reason why they should buy from you over somebody else."

Clients or customers, as they are considering a purchase, have these questions swimming around in their minds:

- What can I count on from this product or service?
- How will my life be better for having spent money on this?
- How long will this product—or the good effects of this service—last?

Reason and Emotion

Benefits are of two types. Type One is rational or tangible benefits, such as a 15 percent cost savings or a new kitchen utensil or a better software program for tracking a household or business budget.

Type Two is emotional and intangible benefits. These are much harder to measure—and, sometimes, much harder for the customer to identify. Emotional benefits have much to do with feelings. For instance, a homeowner will feel pride in his property after a professional landscaping firm has shaped up the front lawn. A family will feel safe after a state-of-the-art security system has been installed. A business person will feel confident and peaceful once a highly reputable and expert CPA firm has taken over the books.

When you can truly put yourself in your customer's place and look back upon the product or service you offer from the viewpoint of the purchaser, you will be equipped to identify both the tangible and the intangible benefits of whatever you have to sell. Then, with a healthy dose of creativity, you should try to capture in words the feelings a client or customer may experience as the purchase is being made. Be sure to hint at this emotional side of the buying experience as you convey in words and images to potential purchasers the benefits of doing business with you:

"Breathe easy now—your financial planning needs are being met."

"When you'd like to see your business expand by leaps and bounds, try Gateway Marketing Consultants."

"The one store where books, records, gifts and great food all come together."

By identifying how you and your company are unique, then translating that into words and pictures that depict benefits to customers or clients, you may soon have more business than you can handle.

There is a vitality, a life force, an energy, a quickening, that is translated through you into action, and because there is only one of you in all time, this expression is unique.

— Martha Graham

Bring ideas in and entertain them royally, for one of them may be the king.

— Mark Van Doren

The sole purpose of business is service. The sole purpose of advertising is explaining the service which business renders.

— Leo Burnett, founder, Leo Burnett Advertising

You have to have your heart in your business and the business in your heart.

— Thomas J. Watson, Sr., founder, IBM

One of the secrets of life is to make stepping stones out of stumbling blocks.

— Jack Penn

Advertising is any communication that seeks to influence, persuade, inform or eductate the consumer—any commercial message about the brand that touches the consumer. That's advertising.

— Shelly Lazarus, chairman,
  Ogilvy & Mather Advertising

You may be disappointed if you fail, but you are doomed if you don't try.

— Beverly Sills

CHAPTER 21

**Promote the Benefits
and Increase Your Sales**

Defining and Selling the Sizzle (Not the Steak)

In the factory we make cosmetics; in the store we sell hope.

— Charles Revson, founder of Revlon

Marketing materials, including workshops and courses, frequently talk about "selling the benefits, not the features." Even after you've had some of the lectures and have taken notes, you may still find yourself asking, "How do I define those benefits? And how can I best get them across to my customers and prospects?" Good questions. Let's dive in and see if some expanded definitions and illustrations can help.

Typically, people who are interested in your product or service are looking for positive change. Some examples: The furniture is threadbare or overstuffed or just the wrong shape or color, and they want some that fits their current taste or desire. The last oil change they did was too expensive or the oil that was used doesn't seem to be high-performance, and this time they want more value—or better results.

Personally, I like to distinguish among features,

results, and benefits/feelings. See if making those distinctions doesn't help you, too.

People don't just acquire a new car; they want a better feeling while they are driving. They'll get that feeling if their car's features result in its holding the road more securely, taking the curves more smoothly, or getting more acceleration on the upgrade. Such performance will engender a better feeling while they drive. They'll also feel better about themselves if the car looks good to others as they park in front of a restaurant and join a group of friends for dinner.

Using Good Feelings

The concept of "good feelings" is itself a helpful key to understanding what sales professionals mean when they talk about selling the benefits. Top-flight salespeople know how to translate a customer's interest into a cash order: their intuition enables them to focus on just the right feeling that the customer is fishing for when he or she looks over a product, and they can encourage the prospect to believe that that feeling will indeed come with the acquisition.

"Yes, ma'am, that hat does frame your face nicely." Feeling? Pride in appearance.

"Just sink down into that recliner, sir. Feel good?" Feeling? Relief from the tension we carry around with us, maybe even luxuriating in comfort.

"Now look at the logo we've come up with for you: lean and simple, yet striking." Feeling? Hope—hope for a more focused image, hope for increased competitiveness. This logo will convey something essential about our firm and increase our sales.

And people are truly in the market for such benefits. They've got just so much disposable income, and they have to make sharply limited choices in the ways they spend it. The main criterion for making those choices is: How can I acquire something that will satisfy one or more of today's desires?

We Live by and through Desires

Again, let's review some of those desires and see how a product may meet them:

Someone who lives in a dense urban neighborhood doesn't buy a security system; she buys peace of mind. A retail store owner doesn't contract for a new sign; she buys an increased volume of walk-ins. And we all know about chocolate—how, more than its taste or its richness, it's the euphoric vibrations it stirs up in the brain that we're really plunking down our quarters to savor.

Here are some more samplings from an anonymous poem, no doubt penned by some super salesperson somewhere:

"Don't sell me shoes; sell me the pleasure of walking on air.

Don't sell me books; sell me hours of pleasure with new knowledge.

Don't sell me plows; sell me waving fields of green wheat.

Don't sell me things; sell me ideas. . . feelings. . . life. . . happiness."

For your own business now, grab pencil and paper and jot down three items for each product or service you offer: features, benefits, feelings.

For example, an accounting firm:

Features: Deep understanding of tax law, ability to whittle down mountains of receipts and figures rapidly and make sense of it all for the customer.

Results: Accounts that are orderly and accurate and able to stand up to scrutiny from the IRS, along with concrete indications of the business' strengths and weaknesses and its potential for growth.

Benefit/feelings: Relief from the pressure of wrestling with complicated financial figures, plus satisfaction that the finances are under control.

Take a moment and do your own business' offerings.

The more you write during your brainstorming exercise, the better you'll be prepared to make sales presentations, create proposals, and develop marketing materials. Aim for at least half a dozen benefits for each product or service you provide. Then pick your top three. (It's good to choose three, and not just one, because not every customer will necessarily perceive that he or she is getting the same benefits as your other customers. People are different.)

Communicating Your Benefits

All marketing, advertising, and sales is about communicating benefits and then prompting action from current or prospective customers.

Such communication starts with your own crystal-clear awareness of the customer's perspective—hopes for some kind of satisfaction and an understanding of just how your product or service corresponds to those hopes.

Why Testimonials Are Powerful

So do not, in your advertisements and your promotional pieces, try to tell the customer why you think your product works great. Tell them, in words that they themselves might use, how they might describe it as satisfying. This is a prime reason that testimonials from customers are such a powerful form of advertising. And the more random, unposed, and natural those customers are in your video or slide presentation, or the more spontaneous and genuine are the quotes that you use from them in your printed materials, the more believable such communication will be out there in prospectland.

Remember that your customers (or clients) are constantly asking themselves: "What's in it for me (WIIFM)?" The first task of any sales program is to answer that question persuasively. The more effective you are at conveying to them the answer to WIIFM, the more effective your sales program will be—and, consequently, the greater will be the increase in sales.

If a man write a better book, preach a better sermon, or make a better mouse trap than his neighbor, tho' he build his house in the woods, the world will make a beaten path to his door.

— Ralph Waldo Emerson

The more informative your advertising, the more persuasive it will be.

— David Ogilvy, Ogilvy & Mather Advertising

If you are committed to creating value, and if you aren't afraid of the hard times, obstacles become utterly unimportant.

— Candice Carpenter, CEO, ivillage

Plan the sale when you plan the ad.

— Leo Burnett

One person with a belief is equal to a force of ninety-nine who have only interests.

— John Stuart Mill

Aerodynamically the bumble bee shouldn't be able to fly, but the bumble bee doesn't know it, so it goes on flying anyway.

— Mary Kay Ash, founder, Mary Kay Cosmetics

If you don't sell, it's not the product that's wrong, it's you.

— Estee Lauder

Six Steps to Successful Networking

Kind words do not cost much. Yet they accomplish much.

— Blaise Pascal

You walk into the room. It's filled with people, talking in small groups. Buzz, buzz. Slowly you make your way around, stopping first in this clutch of people, then in that, introducing yourself, sharing in the conversation, listening intently to others, then moving on. Welcome to the world of business-to-business networking.

Businesses are built on relationships. That simple sentence provides the rationale behind all the networking efforts going on around the country. You can network almost anywhere, at gatherings specifically set up for that purpose or in other types of meetings, such as new products expositions, conventions—even, on occasion, neighborhood get-togethers. True networkers are ready at every moment, even while waiting for a bus or train.

The object of networking is to develop new business, in other words, to meet potential clients.

Chamber of commerce meetings, various business-after-hours socials, business brunches set up by community college small business centers, and, of course, meetings of various fraternal organizations, such as the Exchange Club, the Optimists, the Moose, the Elks, the Lions Club, and so on, all provide occasions for networking.

Networking groups' close cousin is called the leads groups. Here the idea is that participants will each bring leads for other group members—sort of an all-for-one, one-for-all approach.

Since networking groups and leads groups have become so popular, I thought perhaps you'd like a few pointers to enhance your skills in this fairly new area for building up your business. Not everyone is a natural networker; most of us are somewhat shy and awkward about this sort of thing and actually need to learn how to do it.

Be Interested in Others

Step One. Take a sincere interest in those with whom you are networking. This is hard, if not impossible, to fake. If you are not already a caring person, you have some work to do on yourself in order to become one. But this is the key to successful networking. The phony who's just out for himself, who is insincerely expressing an interest in someone else's business problems or achievements, will eventually be shown up for what he is.

Usually, one of the advantages of dealing with a small firm is what I call "caringness." In contrast to a giant corporation, where you may get passed from person to person via a complicated automated phone answering system, a relative handful of people working almost within earshot of each other tend to become "family." If this has been true for your company, try to communicate some of that "family spirit" as you speak to others about how you and your people serve your clientele. "We try to have fun," you might say, or "We never mind working late when we have to because we enjoy being together so much," or whatever is true for you. One way to show you care about others whom you're meeting is to use their first names. Of course, this means you have to remember names—not always easy, but worth it. One way I remember names is to repeat a person's name silently to myself just after I hear it and then use it deliberately in my first few minutes of conversation with that individual. I also like to use a lot of sentences with "you" and "your" in them to keep the conversation focused on the man or woman I've just met.

Dale Carnegie's Number One rule was "Become genuinely interested in other people." If you've never read this rule in his classic book *How to Win Friends and Influence People*, tonight or tomorrow would be a good time to start. After all, the book sold 15 million copies, so a lot of folks have found it warranted their attention. And they were not wrong.

Ask Questions to Show Interest

Step Two. Ask questions. This is the best way to show people that you are interested in them. Ask about their business, about their family, about their lives. Ask about their hobbies, their goals, their interests. What you ask is not as important as the simple fact that you are asking about something they do or put value in.

Dale Carnegie suggests in his book: "Ask questions that the other man will enjoy answering. Encourage him to talk about himself and his accomplishments. Remember that the man you are talking to is a hundred times more interested in himself and his problems than be is in you and your problems."

The best questions are "open"—that is, they do not invite simple "yes" or "no" answers. My own personal favorites are: "What do you like best about what you're doing?" "How did you get started in. . . ?" A good follow-up question is: "Can you tell me more about. . . ?" The secret is to get people talking about an area where your business might be of service.

Step Three. Listen! Plain and simple—shut your trap and listen. As Voltaire said, "The road to the heart is the ear." Listening is still the great under-tapped skill of the business world. Use it well and you'll never regret it.

Listening is much more than simply hearing. It's not just being quiet. Listening means taking a genuine interest in what the other person is saying and putting forth real effort to understand his or her message. Try, in other words, to get on the other person's wavelength. Most people do not do this when they participate in a conversation; rather, they are usually eager for the other person's message to end so that they can jump in and put in their two cents' worth.

Learn to be an active listener. Keep good eye contact with people while they are talking to you. Smile when appropriate (or express sympathy though another look if that's what's called for), and nod your head to show them you are following their line of thought. Focus yourself on the other person's message and resist distractions. Mentally summarize what you hear being said.

It's good, too, to paraphrase once in a while (not after every third sentence), what you hear the other person saying, something like, "Oh, I see what's been going on in your company. You've been having communication problems between sales and marketing and your product-development people." Or, "Fantastic! That must have been great, to nail down that two-year contract after burning the midnight oil to get your projections together."

Never Interrupt

One important and underemphasized aspect of listening is to resist the temptation to interrupt people, to switch gears or even, presumptuously, to finish their sentences for them. Don't do this!

Pay attention to what Larry King says in his book, *How to Talk to Anyone, Anytime, Anywhere*: "The first rule of conversation is: listen!"

Step Four. Have ready a one-minute commercial for your business. Most people will ask you what you do, especially after you have lent them a very attentive ear for telling their story. So be ready. Their question should cue you to start your commercial rolling. Your informal "script" should include one to three lines that describe what you do, followed by or intermingled with lines that spell out the benefits for your customers or clients. "Me? Well, I come into offices or plants and analyze their computer systems, see what's working well for them, what isn't. When we find problems, we can provide solutions. And we're not beholden to any supplier. We tailor all our purchases to the actual needs of each client. We also guarantee our work 100%."

A good one-minute commercial is one of the most important tools for making your networking expedition a success. It is worth blocking out in advance, even rehearsing to your spouse or a partner or a trusted employee. You want something short but attention-getting. As you compose it, remember the AIDA formula of advertising: attract Attention, generate Interest, create Desire and rouse to Action.

Use these principles in your networking. Grab their attention. Your prospects might meet dozens of other people at the same event, and you want to stand out in their memory. That's why your one-minute commercial needs to describe benefits and results your customers get that they might not get from the competition. Some marketing experts now term this statement your Unique Selling Proposition, a statement that shows how you are unique in your field as well as demonstrating how your uniqueness benefits your customers or clients.

Stoke people's interest in what you do by providing specifics. You cannot get by any more just by talking about "good quality" and "good service"; you must say what exactly your quality and your service comprise—such as a non-breakable toy or a money-back guarantee.

In his book *How to Get Clients*, Jeff Slutsky advises, "The challenge is to create a benefit statement that would grab a prospect's attention. . . . In a conversation, when someone asks you what you do, the benefit statement should cause them to respond with 'No kidding. . . ! How do you do that?' In essence, they're asking you to give a pitch about your product or service."

Be Sure to Exchange Cards

Step Five. Exchange cards. Ask whomever you are talking with for a card. Then offer one of yours. The order is important. You are following through and continuing to express an interest in the other as a first priority. If for any reason your conversation partner does not have a card handy, offer one of yours so that he or she can write a name or number on the back. Be sure to carry a pen.

The exchange of cards complete, you should feel free to excuse yourself from the conversation and move on. You will both be able to get back in touch—which is the idea behind all networking.

Always bring plenty of cards to networking events. Have extras in one of your pockets. I usually try to put my own cards in one pocket and the cards I am receiving in another. This prevents me from giving away one of the cards on which I have written someone else's name and number.

Step Six. Follow-up. You would think this was a no brainer. In actuality, this is the most forgotten or overlooked step of all. It is also the most important. Call each prospect or fax or write or e-mail or whatever they may have suggested. Let all your contacts know that you enjoyed meeting and talking with them, and that you and your firm stand ready to be of service.

Most of the time, following up takes more than one simple phone call. You may start with a call, then follow up a few days later with a letter and a brochure. You might call again, if there has been no invitation to present your product or service, after about an eight-week lapse. It's good to stay in touch periodically, over at least a two-year period, calling or dropping a postcard every four months or so—unless you have received a clear signal that what you have to offer is absolutely of zero interest to your correspondent. In other words, don't be obnoxious, but where there is a prospect of eventual business, don't drop out of sight, either.

As Napoleon once said, "Victory belongs to those who persevere most." Add networking to your marketing efforts, persevere with these six steps, and enjoy unprecedented growth in your own business.

———————

The deepest principle in human nature is the craving to be appreciated.

— William James

To fall in love with yourself is the first secret of happiness. Then if you're not a good mixer you can always fall back on your own company.

— Robert Morley

We live very close together. So, our prime purpose in this life is to help others.

— The Dalai Lama

If you are not using your smile, you're like a man with a million dollars in the bank and no checkbook.

— Les Giblin

Ability may get you to the top, but it takes character to keep you there.

— John Wooden, former basketball coach, UCLA

Section VII

SALES

BUILD YOUR BUSINESS STRONGER—
AND DO IT

23

Optimizing the Process

Six Steps in the Sales Process and How to Improve Your Results

High expectations are the key to everything.

— Sam Walton

Selling remains a mystery to many of us. Just how do great salespeople do what they do?

Some, we know, generate six-figure incomes on their ability to sell. What do they know that the rest of us would like to master? Can anybody learn? Or must one be "a natural"?

If it is true that great sales types are born, not made, maybe there is no way for us to "get there."

Or is there?

Tom Hopkins, author of *How to Master the Art of Selling*, has remarked: ". . . people (may) never climb very high on their potential ladder because they are firm believers in the myth of the natural-born sales wonder."

Let's unveil the sales process—and take some mystery out of it. You will thus see that it is quite approachable, even for those who don't have the super sales personality or those who "just don't like to sell."

Selling can be broken down to six steps:

1) Prepare. It is essential that you know your product or service, your market, your customers and the competition. This means doing your homework on all fronts.

2) Prospect. Leads must be generated, either by you yourself or by someone to whom you assign the task. Otherwise you'll have no one to talk to about your product. Advertising—even if only through an attractive window display—is part of prospecting.

3) Present. How you present your value to the prospects whom you generate is extremely important. The product itself may indeed be great, but a weak presentation will leave you without the sales you need to create adequate profit.

4) Overcome objections. Objections are inevitable—over price ("can't afford it"), timing ("yes, but not now"), and many other issues. Successful salespeople have learned to welcome objections—and overturn them.

5) Close. You must ask for the sale. If you get the words right, and the timing right, your chance of closing will be high.

6) Follow up. The deal won't stay "done" unless you learn to service the account. Most successful enterprises are built on repeat business. And that comes from having satisfied customers.

Each of these steps merits an expanded discussion. So let's take a deeper look.

Prepare

This step could otherwise be called "assessment." It's a taking stock of who you are, what you have to offer, what the market is for your product and services, and who else is selling to that market.

A restaurateur would survey her current menu, staff capabilities, customer flow from one dining period to the next, and what other restaurants in the vicinity were doing. A computer systems consulting firm would list the various services he offered, such as installation, networking, repairing, upgrading, and see how those matched up to the market and what competitors were offering. And so forth.

Pricing of services or of tangible products cannot, of course, be left out. Other elements to note would be availability or timeliness, and willingness to correct any mistakes (money-back guarantees, replacements, credits on future orders, etc.).

It is best, of course, to write everything down. Items surveyed just "in the head" have a way of becoming nebulous. Once all relevant aspects of your products and services are down on paper, and compared with market demand and with competitors' offerings, a very concrete picture will emerge.

It is this concrete picture that you need to move on to the next step.

Overall, the most important element in preparation is the deepening of belief in your product or service. You need to cultivate a conviction that what you have to offer is valuable and of high quality.

This conviction will come through in everything you say or do as you move through the remaining steps in the process.

Prospect

Prospecting is the label we give to generating "leads" for your business. The leads are individuals or organizations to whom you can present your products and/or services. Here are some of the most common methods of generating leads:

- Advertising (print, broadcast, billboards)
- Direct mail
- Trade show booths
- Telemarketing
- Cold calling
- Networking
- Leads groups.

To learn what prospecting methods might work best for you, it is a good idea to study what other people in your industry are doing. Try to apply the best practices of people you identify as successful.

Each industry, I have found, has its own favorites: real estate agents, for instance, favor newspaper advertising and signs on vehicles and in front of homes they have listed; a home air filter company might rely heavily on telemarketing; while a manufacturer's rep may lean heavily on trade shows and cold calling.

Next, look at other industries. What are people in sectors totally different from yours doing to generate prospects? Remember, there is no "right answer" here. You are simply trying to broaden your view of the selling process. When you uncover a method popular in some other industry, ask yourself, "Is there a good chance that could work with my product or service?" If your answer to yourself is "yes," and others whom you trust for advice concur, give that approach a try. Be willing to copy successful approaches, whether from your own sector or from a completely different sector.

Don't forget to revisit methods that have worked for you in the past. If networking through organizations such as the chamber of commerce and a fraternal club such as

Elks brought you three new clients for your advertising agency last year, chances are good that those fields are still fertile.

An extremely important aspect of prospecting is the issue of "qualifying." It does you no good at all to generate prospects who, in truth, will not be able to afford to pay for what you are selling. Ask yourself these questions: Does the person I am talking to on the phone or in person have the authority to buy?

Is this person or organization willing to make the financial commitment that my product or service requires? Can they be trusted to pay everything they will owe, and in a timely fashion? Are they in the market to buy, or are they just window shopping for some future occasion?

In *Prospecting—The Key to Sales Success*, Viriden J. Thornton lists these characteristics of a qualified prospect. Someone who

• has a need or a problem that can be met or resolved by purchasing your products/services,

• sees the need or problem and is willing to take action,

• is willing to consider your products/services as a solution to his or her problems or needs,

• can afford to purchase your products/services,

• has the authority to spend money to make the purchase.

It makes no sense to spin your wheels chasing people who are either not ready to buy, don't have the authority to buy, or cannot be trusted to fulfill their obligations. The only prospect, in a sense, is a qualified prospect.

A great way to qualify prospects is to assign a letter grade based upon the criteria above. Call "A" Prospects the best and "C" prospects the poorest. Then spend most of your time on your "A" list and try to convert your "B's" into "A's." Spend as little time as possible on your "C's."

With effective lead generation and sound qualifying, you are ready to move on to the next step.

Present

The heart of the sales process is presentation. Pay careful attention! This step breaks down into two parts: 1) Designing the presentation and 2) Delivering the presentation.

Designing what and how you will present is an art in itself. Ideally, the presentation should be built around benefits that you and your product or service offer the customer that are better than what they might get elsewhere. They may be better because they are higher in quality, have special features, are more easily available, priced better, or come with guarantees and follow-up not matched by anyone else.

In some fashion you should try to position yourself as unique in your market. The benefits, then, are sometimes called a Unique Selling Proposition (USP).

It's also important to remind yourself that your prospects are always asking themselves: "Is this a good match for what I need?" In other words, "What's in it for me?" (abbreviated WIIFM). All sales presentations succeed or fail according to how they respond to this key prospect question.

After your design is complete, memorize the entire presentation. Practice it until you know it by heart and can go through it naturally, not in a stiff rote fashion. Having the presentation down pat will free up your energy for other aspects of presenting, such as listening and meeting prospect objections.

When delivering your presentation, remember to listen as well as to talk. Too many sales are lost because the enthusiastic salesperson talks a prospect to death. This can happen even when you feel the presentation is going well—and so you just keep talking. You actually need to leave room for your prospect to raise objections—reasons not to buy.

That is because to close a sale you will undoubtedly have to counter any objections they raise. If they raise none at all, and they are qualified to buy, you are pretty much home free. If they do raise objections, you need to build a case for the value of your product/service over and above the objections (we will cover this in the next section).

Listen especially closely for why a prospect wants to buy. That is the most important thing to hear. Surprisingly, the prospect's reason might not be the same as the reason you are pitching to them.

Nonetheless, pick up on their reason and reinforce it for them. For instance, if you run a paint store, you might be geared up to tout the merits of the great variety of brands and tints you offer, including quite a range of prices. For the prospect, however, the most important thing may be that your store is just three blocks from their house and if they need more paint as their work progresses, they can pop in quickly to pick it up.

Overcome Objections

Overcoming objections is a high art form. People who develop this skill will never be short of business.

Every prospect who decides not to buy has one, or several, objections. Your job is to identify those objections and overcome them. Some people will come right out and tell you their objection to buying. Others will camouflage their main objection behind lesser or even trivial objections. Others will not give you an objection at all, just back off and decline to buy.

It's best to actually encourage objections. Get them on the table, so to speak. This is a natural part of the buying process and you should not allow it to intimidate or discourage you from your mission of selling.

The most common objection is: "It costs too much." Or: "I can't afford it." It is best to be aware and expect this objection. Price often turns out to to be the major hurdle to completing a sale.

One simple way to address the "costs too much" objection is to find out what the prospect is comparing your product or service to. Just ask, "Compared to what?" If you are showing a woman a $60 perfume and she raises the issue of price, you might inquire whether she ever spends $60 on a dress. The perfume, you might suggest, will last as long as the dress and may prove equally important in helping her feel fresh and attractive.

Most of the time when people say, "That costs too much," they have not yet heard enough value for the price you are asking. Your job then is to communicate more about the value of the product or service, detail the benefits and the USP. Explain how what you have to offer will make their life easier, more satisfying, more fun, safer, or more convenient.

It is actually easier to head off objections than to wait until the prospect mentions them. For example, if your roofing business charges more than the competition, you might say, "We decided early on in our business that we wanted to provide the highest quality roof on the market. That way people might pay a little more in the beginning, but they will have years of trouble free and comfortable living under that roof." Or: "I believe that it's easier to explain a slightly higher cost than to apologize for a low quality and consequent problems for years and years."

Of course you won't succeed in overcoming the objections of all prospects. It's more like batting averages.

If you can hit 400—that is, sell 4 out of 10 prospects—you may be doing very well indeed.

Close

The close is the step most people fear the most. If you have done the first four steps well, however, the close should feel fairly natural. The better prepared you are, the higher the qualify of your prospects, the more developed your presentation, the more skillful you are at handling objections, the easier will be the close.

The most obvious thing about the close—and sometimes the forgotten thing—is to ask for the sale.

In one form or another, you must finally confirm that the prospect will buy what you are selling, be that a tangible product or a service. Virden J. Thornton describes this process in his book *Closing—A Process, Not a Problem.* He outlines six steps for closing:

Step 1: Build rapport and trust.

Step 2: Capture your prospect's attention.

Step 3: Probe for problems, opportunities, needs, values, attitudes and lifestyles.

Step 4: Demonstrate your products or services based on specific needs.

Step 5: Ask trial closing questions and answer objections.

Step 6: Ask for the sale.

This is a complete system for closing. On another level,

it spans the elements of the entire selling process.

Professional salespeople do call upon a number of closing techniques. To highlight a few:

Assumptive close: You proceed as though you are assuming they will buy. For instance, you get out the forms
to write up the order, or you get a box for the product. If
he or she wants to back off, they will have to speak up
and actually tell you, "No, I'm not buying."

Ownership close: You get the prospect to envision owning the product or receiving the service, imagining how it
will be to view the Disney channel on cable television or
where they will place the new recliner in the family room.

Choice/options close: "Would you like this dress in blue
or tan?" "Do you need installation immediately or can it
wait till after the weekend?"

Summary close: You recap all the product's features,
asking for the customer's agreement as you go. "With your
new vacuum cleaner, with all these attachments, you won't
hesitate to tackle any rug or floor cleaning project, will
you?"

Little decision close: You invite the prospect to make a
series of little decisions instead of the big decision to buy
or not. This car comes with a three-year warranty, but of
course that's your choice. Would you want it with or without power windows? We also have this same model as a
demonstrator from last year if you'd like to save even more
on a car that's been driven only eight or nine thousand
miles. . . .

Order blank close: Let the customer fill in the order
blank with the initial basic information to start the sale
process.

Must-act-now close: We've all heard the close where
we have to buy within a certain timeframe (Sale ends this

Monday!) or lose the deal. Be careful when using this close, however, because everyone has heard it over and over.

Puppy dog close: Once you get the kids to hold the dog, puppies sell themselves. Some products are also like that—sporting goods and toys, for instance.

Incentive/premium close: Near the end of the sales process, you add something that is valuable—a bonus how-to booklet, for example—to sweeten the deal and prompt the prospect to buy right now.

Ben Franklin close: You make the deal clearer and more attractive by listing the pros and cons on a sheet of paper. This close is especially effective if you can get the prospect to make the list and they come up with a lot more pros than cons.

Ask for the order close: Ask for the sale with a simple question such as, "Shall I wrap it up for you?"

Zig Ziglar's book *Secrets of Closing the Sale* has many more techniques if you are interested in expanding your repertoire.

Whenever closing, and no matter what close you are using, focus on the benefits to the customer. This will make any close more effective. Remember, too, that not everyone is ready to buy after just one conversation. People often need time to come to a decision. Let the process unfold at the customer's pace.

Finally, don't ever force a sale. It may seem like a success at the moment, but sticking someone with a product or service they do not truly desire will likely come back to haunt you. Better forgo a sale than to create an unhappy, dissatisfied customer. Thus, high-pressure sales may even hurt your business in the long run, as dissatisfied customers tend to spread the word of their unhappiness far and wide.

Follow Up

After you've made the sale, why bother? Follow-up is the easiest step to leave out. However, follow-up is the key to repeat business. You follow up with the customer to see how they are doing and to remind them of other products and services you have to offer.

It matters little how you put the question—phone call, questionnaire or person-to-person—just that you do ask.

Have their expectations been met? Is the product or service doing what they hoped it would? If they have complaints, what are they, and is it something you may be able to fix?

These are important questions. It will be difficult to achieve long-term success if you do not get affirmative answers to such queries. Keep in mind that when a customer brings up a problem, it is a good thing. It is much worse for there to be problems and you not to be aware of them. Having someone evoke a problem with the product or service you sold also allows you to develop a solution. It will also help you re-engineer the product or retailor the service, which may be vital for continuing success.

A happy or very satisfied customer is much more likely to refer other prospects to you. And this is the greatest benefit to you of following up.

Look back over the six steps. Which are your strong points? Your weak points? Work on building up the areas where you need to bolster your skills. A little self knowledge here will go a long way—as will the effort to improve where improvement is needed. Success in business requires working to get better—all the time!

Some of my favorite books on sales include

How to Master the Art of Selling by Tom Hopkins, Tom Hopkins International, Inc., 1982.

Zig Ziglar's Secrets of Closing the Sale, by Zig Ziglar, Berkeley Books, 1984.

Nido Qubein's Professional Selling Techniques by Nido Qubein, Berkeley Books, 1983.

Customer-Focused Selling by Nancy J. Stephens with Bob Adams, Adams Media Corporation, 1996.

Closing—A Process, Not A Problem by Virden J. Thornton, Crisp Publications, 1995.

Prospecting—The Key to Sales Success by Virden J. Thorton, Crisp Publications, 1994.

———————

It is our duty as men and women to proceed as though the limits of our abilities do not exist.

— Pierre Teilhard de Chardin

We are all salesmen every day of our lives. We are selling our ideas, our plans, our enthusiasms to those with whom we come in contact.

— Charles M. Schwab

The word impossible is not in my dictionary.

— Napoleon Bonaparte

In selling as in medicine, prescription before diagnosis is malpractice.

— John Naisbitt, author, **Megatrends**

The outstanding leaders of every age are those who set up their own quotas and constantly exceed them.

— Thomas J. Watson, founder IBM

I would never have amounted to anything were it not for adversity. I was forced to come up the hard way.

— James C. Penney

Whatever you do, do it with all your might. Work at it, early and late, in season and out of season, not leaving a stone unturned, and never deferring for a single hour that which can be done just as well as now.

— P.T. Barnum

Success seems to be largely a matter of hanging on after others have let go.

— William Feather

CHAPTER

24

Seek Out Client Needs to Build Your Business

Cultivate the Art of Asking Good Questions

Judge a man by his questions rather than by his answers.

— Voltaire

What are your needs? Your goals? Would you like to learn some ways to fulfill them both? If I could show you a few simple questions you can ask prospective clients to insure that your business grows, would that be worth a few minutes of your time?

Have I sold you yet on reading this chapter?

Here is the bottom line. Most, if not all, businesses are driven by sales. And even though you may prefer to think of yourself as an accountant, an inventor, or a cappucino-bar proprietor, the truth is that you are also a salesperson. Or you'd better be if you want to not only survive, but also thrive in your own venture.

How successful we become depends to a considerable degree on our effectiveness in selling your products or services. We can't simply look over our shoulder at someone else we've brought on board to "handle" sales. Our sales volume still depends heavily on ourselves as own-

171

ers, on our personalities, drive, enthusiasm, and motivation to sell.

Do I hear moans and groans from some of you reading this? Perhaps comments such as, "That's not me, not my shtick. I'm a manager, not a salesperson." Or, "I design clothes. I can hire other people to sell what I design." Or, "I have valuable consulting skills. People are just going to have to recognize the value of what I can do for them. I'm not going to go pushing myself on people or get into doing a sales pitch."

Not to worry. I'm not here to coach on pitching or on badgering people through cold calling or hoked-up surveys. I am here instead to show you that your best sales tactic is your quite simply taking a sincere interest in your prospects and their own personal and business needs and goals.

Ask and You Shall Receive

The best way to show such an interest is through cultivating the art of asking good questions.

There's general agreement among such popular experts on motivation and sales as Zig Ziglar, Charles D. Brennan, Jr. and Tom Hopkins that most sales efforts involve entirely too much telling about products and services. What's missing is an adequate amount of *asking* about client needs and *listening carefully* to client responses.

Rather than encouraging you to be at all "pushy," I'd like to help you focus on becoming more inquisitive (in discreet, tasteful ways) and developing your *listening skills*. Those are the ways to heightened sales—which translates into a growing business.

An old adage applies here: "You were born with two ears and only mouth for a reason—you should listen twice as much as you speak."

Experienced, successful salespeople have all learned this lesson. They know full well that their sales will go up as they improve upon the content and delivery of questions to determine customer needs and desires. After all, sales is a service business. You as a salesperson—whether behind the counter in a jeans-and-T-shirt boutique or out networking at receptions—are there to help identify and resolve the problems that your customers and prospects are facing. That absolutely demands that you come up with the right questions.

The second step in the process is to know how and when to lay back and just listen to the responses. Only through skillful listening can you determine what it is that a prospect would actually like you to provide in the way of products or services.

Kinds of Questions to Ask

If asking questions works so well, how can we learn what kinds of questions to ask?

First, believe me, there are indeed *bad* questions and also bad ways of asking questions. And these you'll want to learn to avoid. Let's take a for-instance.

Say you have a special occasion coming up and you need a shirt or blouse. Armed with cash, or a credit card, you venture into a clothing store at your local mall. As you enter the store, a well-meaning sales associate greets you and asks innocently, "May I help you?"

What's your instant reflex going to be? Even though you are on a buying mission, you probably are going to tell the associate, "No, I'm just looking."

Even when we have a desire to buy, most of us still give that reflex answer. But the reason we do so is not any sudden second guessing of our purchasing mission, but rather the kind of question we've been asked. It simply is not a very good question.

Here are some much better approaches:

"Hi. Welcome to. . . (name of store). I wonder if I can help direct you to any particular section of our store?"

"What clothing items are you most interested in looking over today?"

"Is there any special clothing need you're trying to fill at the moment?"

"Would you mind telling me what kind of styles or colors you especially like, and then I'll know better where to direct your attention in our store."

"Have you noticed that many of our clothes have been reduced or are on closeout today?"

Some types of questions should be avoided. Those that are too blunt, for instance—"Why not sign here right now?" Those that are too indiscreet or too offensive—"You sure do look as if you could use our weight-control program. Why not give us a try?" Or questions that bash the competition—"Isn't it easy to see how superior our product is over what you've been used to?"

It's also important to distinguish between two types of questions—closed questions and open-ended questions.

A closed question is one that can be answered with a simple "yes" or "no." This type of question offers limited information and is usually designed to engage the prospect in a process that will lead toward a sale.

Good closed questions are designed to maximize the chances of receiving a "yes" response from the prospect. Recently I heard one of the best closed questions I'd ever come across from a salesperson at a shipping company. He asked me this: "If I could show you a way to save money on shipping while maintaining your present high level of service to your customers, would you be interested in getting more information?"

How could anyone say no to that?

Another type of closed question gives the prospect a choice between two or move answers: Would you rather have this equipment delivered on Tuesday or on Thursday? If you were to sign up for our hair transplant surgery, would you be able to handle it in one or two large payments, or would you prefer our credit plan spaced out over two years?

Open-ended questions are designed to evoke much more than a "yes" or "no" answer. They seek to get the client or prospect talking about their own preferences, desires, needs, or constraints.

One of the most important things to learn about a prospect is why he or she is even interested in exploring what you have to offer in products or services—not why *you* think they should be interested but why *they*, within the context of their own reality, are curious or interested.

While some people will come straight out and tell you why they are interested, a surprising number will not. When you sense that this is the case, you have a perfect opportunity to ask, "Can you give me an idea of what specifically about our product appeals to you?" or, "What is it about the services we offer that seems to respond to a need or a goal that you have?"

More Ways to Turn Prospects into Customers

Here are some other sample questions that fit different occasions in the process of turning prospects into customers:

- "Have you ever tried (name a feature of your product or service)?"

- "Would you consider using. . . ?"
- "Would you agree with me that. . . " (and name something you know the prospect will agree with—his business would grew faster with a concerted professional marketing effort or her store would attract more customers if a professional did the window displays, etc.)
- "Can I give you some more useful details about how our product (or service) operates?"
- "How can we help you afford our product (or service) since you obviously seem to have a keen interest in taking advantage of it?"
- "Could I put our offer to you in writing and back it up with a guarantee for parts and service?"

If you would like to go deeper into this topic, I suggest you read *Ziglar on Selling—The Ultimate Handbook for Complete Sales*, by Zig Ziglar (Ballantine Books, 1991), *How to Master the Art of Selling*, by Tom Hopkins (Warner Books, 1982) and *Sales Questions that Close the Sale*, by Charles D. Brennan, Jr. (AmA, 1994).

I've learned from experience that the greater part of our happiness or misery depends on our dispositions and not our circumstances.

— Martha Washington, first First Lady

So what do we do? Anything. Something. So long as we just don't sit there. If we screw it up, start over. Try something else. If we wait until we've satisfied all the uncertainies, it may be too late.

— Lee Iacocca, former Chairman, Chrysler Corp.

Intelligent Negotiation—
Your Key to Sales Success

Nothing astonishes men so much as common sense and
plain dealing.

> — Ralph Waldo Emerson

Who hasn't seen the line used in advertising for Chester
Karrass, a prominent sales trainer: "You don't get what
you deserve—you get what you negotiate"?

For those of you who may have associated negotiating
strictly with bringing warring factions to a peace pact or
coming to terms with fired-up union leaders threatening
to shut down a whole industrial sector, it's time to re-
examine your assumptions. Negotiating is a mainstream
instrument for advancing your enterprise, almost on a
day-to-day basis.

In addition, if you don't have some mastery of negotiating techniques, you may be the unwitting object of someone else's using them on you—with virtually zero awareness on your part of how you may be being manipulated.

It is therefore strongly in your interest to learn how to
negotiate.

The truth is that, though you may not have been

using the term "negotiating," you have been engaged in
the process for a long time, probably ever since you
wheedled a sugar-frosted pacifier from your mom while
she was on a supermarket expedition with you.

In *Selling through Negotiation*, author Homer B. Smith
says: "Professional salespeople have always been negotiators, whether they realized it or not. All of the selling skills,
product knowledge, attitudes and working habits developed during a salesperson's career are aimed at developing greater negotiating power for the salesperson when in
a sales situation."

Awareness is the key to effective negotiating. To be
fully aware, you need to know how the pros negotiate—
and how you may counter their moves. Otherwise, you
are likely to be had, over and over again, with possibly
disastrous consequences for your small business.

Negotiating involves what some people call "gambits."
These are preemptive strikes, as in chess strategy. Many
of these gambits are used daily by people who have little
or no formal training in negotiation; they are also used by
people who have learned them in a classroom.

Capitalize on the Most Common Gambits

Good Guy/Bad Guy. Perhaps the most common gambit, its effectiveness is reduced because many consumers
have heard of it. It consists of having two people negotiate
with you, rather than just one, and of those two, having
one pretend to side with you while the other seemingly
plays hardball. For instance, the floor sales person will be
very sympathetic to your offer or objections to a product,
while the sales manager, called to the scene, will offer
stout resistance to price flexibility, discounting, or other
special arrangements.

The counter to this gambit is to say to both of them, "I know you two are working together and this opposition between you is artificial. . . trumped up." This removes the illusion of having one salesman "on your side." Most of the time, saying this is not even necessary as long as you realize that two people are using the good guy/bad guy gambit on you. Simply adjust your reactions accordingly.

Higher Authority. There you are, more or less finishing a deal with someone you believe has the authority to sign a contract with you, and then your counterpart says, "Well, I wish I could agree to all this just on my say-so. But I'll have to take this to my boss (or board of directors, supervisor, partner, etc., etc.)" Whether we are trying to sell something or have been negotiating to buy something, this ploy really takes the wind out of our sails.

When other, perhaps less favorable, contractual terms come down to you, you may feel you just have to go along, because you're never going to meet the "higher authority" face to face anyway. And you may thus conclude a deal that is not nearly so much to your advantage as the one you thought you had agreed upon.

One good counter to the higher-authority gambit is to say, "Look, why don't you recommend to your boss (or board of directors, supervisor, partner, etc., etc.), what you think will be in your firm's best interests? Why don't you just tell me what you plan to recommend, and let's negotiate around that? After all, you're one of their top reps. I'm sure they'll give you some latitude to negotiate, and I'm sure they listen to your recommendations on pricing and specs, don't they?"

Nibble (or Salami). The idea here is to negotiate the way you munch on a salami—a little at a time. Salespersons who continually ask for small and seemingly insig-

nificant items or concessions can creep up on the prospect and then get a "yes" for the big sale. Insurance companies and banks often do this by getting you to sign up
for virtually free life or burial insurance and then come
back to you constantly to get you to increase your "guarantee of a carefree future." Or credit card prospectors will
get you to accept their card by offering you an initial interest rate so low you'd feel like an idiot refusing the card.
The catch: After six months, the rate will rise to prime
plus six points.

The counterattack to the "nibble gambit" requires that
you first recognize the game being played. Bargain with
such negotiators, if you like, but bargain with your eyes
wide open.

Anticlimax. Once a sale is "complete," prospects often
let down their guard. They don't realize that a vendor may
be trying to get them to buy even more. Car dealers do
this all the time. You have just spent hours negotiating
price and options and then, when you think everything is
signed, sealed and all but delivered, the salesman may
ask you if you want the rustproofing and the three-year
warranty on parts and labor. Both of these items are highly
profitable for the dealer. Because the prospect thinks the
negotiations have been concluded and is relaxed, he or
she is likely to say "yes."

Some Additional Negotiating Tips

- Beware of "standard" contracts. There may be nothing at all standard about the contract that is being offered to you.
- Be a "reluctant buyer." Such a pose will always work
better for you. Being too eager to conclude any deal is
sure to tip the negotiations in favor of the other party.

- Look for false intentions. People may try to convince you that their priority in the negotiating process is one thing, when actually what is most important to them is something different. A roofing contractor may tell you that if you sign now, you'll be included in a special for the street, since some of your neighbors have already put down deposits. In fact, your signature may be the first one they've gotten on your street.
- Always be willing to walk away from a deal. You are at a big disadvantage if you just can't walk away.

While it's true that in some instances you may find yourself negotiating with someone misrepresenting a product or service or sticking you with an inflated price or unreasonable terms, your best long-term strategy is to claim the high road of honor, fairness, and reliability.

Ideally, your approach to negotiations ought to be win-win. This means that whether you are the seller or the buyer, both you and your counterpart will come away with something you want and something that is worth the money or effort you put behind the trading process.

When I go to see my marketing consultant, she gives me her best advice based on what she hears me reporting as needs, and I pay her an hourly fee that I have decided is fair for the quality of service she provides. We both win. If she were to listen to me with only half an ear, or get slack in trying to match marketing techniques with my particular situation, then I would be the loser. If I tried and succeeded in chipping away at her fee until she ended up cheating herself for not spending time with other clients who would pay full freight, she would be the loser. The happy medium is to reach an accord on a deal that suits both parties.

There are many excellent books on negotiation. A few of my favorites:

Roger Dawson's Secrets of Power Negotiating, by Roger Dawson (Career Press, 1995).

Everything's Negotiable, by Eric William Skopec and Laree S. Kiely (AmA, 1994).

Selling Through Negotiation, by Homer B. Smith (Marketing Education Associates, 1988).

You Can Negotiate Anything, by Herb Cohen (Lyle Stuart, 1980).

Nothing gives one person so much advantage over another as to remain cool and unruffled under all circumstances.

— Thomas Jefferson

My philosophy is that not only are you responsible for your life, but doing the best at this moment puts you in the best place for the next moment.

— Oprah Winfrey

Many persons have a wrong idea of what constitutes true happiness. It is not attained through self-gratification but through fidelity to a worthy purpose.

— Helen Keller

We may affirm absolutely that nothing great in the world has been accomplished without passion.

— Hegel

The superior man thinks always of virtue.

— Confucius

chapter 26

**Better to Ask Them
Than to Lose Them**

Do You Know What Your Customers Really Want?

We are here on earth to do good to others.
What the others are here for, I don't know.

— W.H. Auden

Michael LeBoeuf, in his book *How to Win Customers and Keep Them for Life*, tells the story of a small boy who enters a telephone booth at a pharmacy and, within earshot of the drugstore manager, engages in the following conversation. "Hello. . . is this the Kingsley residence? I understand you have an opening for a part-time gardener. What? You've just hired somebody? Well, is he working out? Are you satisfied with how he cuts the grass and tends the flowers and trims the hedges? You are. . . ? Do you plan on keeping him? Oh. . . I see. Well, I'm sorry the job has been filled, but I'm glad you're getting such good service. Goodbye."

As the boy leaves the booth, the drugstore manager stops him. "I couldn't help overhearing your conversation there, Tommy. Excuse me, it's none of my business I know, but aren't you the boy the Kingsleys just hired to take care of their yard?"

Tommy replies, "That's right. I was just calling to check on how I'm doing out there."

The lesson here for customer service is an important one. It might be summed up in an axiom attributed to Daniel R. Scoggin, president and CEO of TGIFridays's Inc.: "The only way to know how customers see your business is to look at it through their eyes." Or, to use one of the buzz phrases of the 90s, "Perception is everything."

Feedback from your customers, old, new, and potential, is key to answering the question, "How are we doing?" And negative feedback, the kind that tells you why people are dissatisfied with your product or service, has especially strong value, even though all of us hate to hear how we may be missing the mark.

In his book, LeBoeuf cites some powerful statistics bearing on customer relations. I hope they will serve as a dash of cold water to splash all of you awake who may be resistant—or just lazy—regarding the need to explore customer attitudes toward how you do business.

Facts on Customer Satisfaction

• The average business hears from only 4 percent (1 in 25) of its dissatisfied customers. The other 96 percent just go away and never come back.

• A typical dissatisfied customer will tell eight to ten people about why he or she felt shortchanged by a product or service.

• The average business spends six times more money to attract new customers than it does to keep its standing customers.

• Seven out of ten complaining customers will do business with you again if YOU receive their complaint. Ninety-five percent will stay with you if you solve the problem on the spot.

LeBoeuf charges that the overwhelming majority of American companies fail miserably in the area of measuring customer satisfaction—even though, when surveyed, they all declare this area to be of critical importance. Why don't more businesses undertake to learn just how customers regard what they produce or tender as a service? The answer most frequently given, LeBoeuf says, is, "We don't know how to do such measuring."

Yes, of course customer service surveying is more nebulous than, say, measuring cash flow, return on investment, gross, and net revenues, and other indices that can be computed in hard dollars. Yet any accountant can tell you that there is no such thing as absolutely precise information and that all those "hard" numbers aren't always that perfect either.

"When it comes to winning and keeping customers, a company without a well planned system of customer feedback is burying its head in the sand," LeBoeuf says, and he quotes Dr. Robert Anthony as noting: "If you stick your head in the sand, one thing is for sure: You'll get your rear kicked."

Use Your Small Business Advantage

Small businesses have the advantage of being naturally closer to their customers than the behemoth companies. If you own a flower and gift shop, you, the owner, are likely to be in the store 80% of the operating hours and deal personally, face to face, with most of the people who come in searching for just the right bouquet to say "I'm sorry" or "Let's celebrate." If you are an accountant in solo practice, you'll see 100% of your clients 100% of the time. And so forth. Therefore, you can simply ask, in casual and colloquial fashion, at an appropriate moment (such as when an exchange is ending and you're ready to say goodbye) how your client or customer has been perceiving your product or service. Here are a few sample questions you can use for such informal surveys:

• Tell me, how are we doing in measuring up to your expectations?

• What would you say are the areas where we need to improve how we do things?

• Would you say our prices are low, high, or about right for the value you're receiving?

Wait until the customer or client has taken leave before you jot down some of the comments you received. Then keep those comments on file along with those of other customers. Here and there you'll have an outspoken or over-demanding client whose expectations might be next to impossible to fulfill. But focus on the broad responses you get from doing such informal surveying. What you pay the most attention to are the preponderant attitudes.

Additional Ways to Survey Clients

There are two other ways of surveying your clientele, both useful. The first is with a written questionnaire, such as those used by restaurants and hotels. A comment card, for example, can be found in any Seven-Eleven store and mailed to the parent Southland Corporation. The card is short and to the point. That's important because too much detail will cause customers to balk at spending the time and effort to fill out your survey.

Written surveys lend themselves to asking customers to rank you on a scale of one to five. Or you can simply use terms such as "Always," "Usually," "Sometimes," "Infrequently," "Never" or "Excellent," "Very Good," "Good,"

"Fair," "Poor." Such calibration of responses is helpful because it may give you harder data than you can get from the informal, face-to-face surveying.

The second additional way of surveying is by telephone. Although they are the most expensive form of surveying, telephone polls will give you the best overall picture. People responding to face-to-face surveys will often temper their responses and may not be completely honest, because they don't want to upset the interviewer—especially if the interviewer is also the owner of the business. Written questionnaires, research shows, tend to be filled out mainly by people who either strongly dislike or strongly appreciate your product or service, not by the broad band of customers in between. So long as you keep the survey short and to the point, and promise at the outset not to take up much of the respondent's time, you will get good cooperation over the phone from a broad range of your clients—and probably the most honest answers.

• Overall, how would you rate the quality of our service?
• How would you rate the appearance of our facilities?
• How well do we understand your special needs?
• How much confidence do you have in our products or services?
• How quickly do we respond to your requests?
• How accessible are we when YOU need to contact us?
• How helpful and polite are we in dealing with you?
• How willing would you be to recommend us to your friends?

Whatever you do, LeBoeuf insists, do not let customers quit your business without knowing the reason why. Telephone them or politely drop in on them and do whatever is reasonable to get them back or at least come to some understanding of how they feel your product or service fell short.

Once you receive feedback that is broad enough and specific enough to show you what customers perceive as weak spots, it's critical that you put the information to work toward improving appearances, features, quality, or price of what you have to sell. List the problem areas in order of gravity and circle the most serious ones. Then establish priorities for how you will tackle the problems, starting with the most serious, and get to work!

Handling Customer Complaints Well

In their book *Delivering Knock Your Socks Off Service*, Kristen Anderson and Ron Zemke offer a six-point approach for handling customer complaints:

1. Apologize. "I'm really sorry that this item did not work out for you." "I'm so sorry we were late with that delivery and caused you problems." "I regret that our instructions were not clear enough for you."

2. Listen and empathize. "Sounds like you had a lot of trouble with that appliance." "It certainly must have been disappointing when you found there were pieces missing from the package and you couldn't finish the assembly." "Our coffee usually gets rave reviews, but that day our water filter was giving us problems and I'm sure you and our other customers suffered for it."

3. Fix the problem quickly and fairly. This is, I realize, more often easier said than done. Solutions may range from returning money on a purchase; offering a substitute item; handling a repair under warranty; redoing a service product, such as a marketing survey or news release, gratis; or whatever is specific to your business. The bottom line is that customers want what they had expected to receive in the first place.

4. Offer atonement. "Please accept this discount card

good for any item in the store." "Your next meal here is on the house," and so on.

5. Keep your promises. You need to recover the customer's trust, which has been damaged or temporarily lost. Don't go overboard and promise the moon. Remember that wonderful business axiom: Under-promise and over-deliver. You won't make any unhappy customers that way.

6. Follow up. Check to be sure that, in the customer's perception, adequate amends have been made and the level of service is back up to expectations. "Everything working okay now on that blow dryer, Mrs. Watkins?" "Coffee okay this week, Terry?"

A very few customers may be truly difficult, occasionally even abusive to you in spite of all your best efforts. You should NOT simply stand in the line of fire of someone who is using profanity or a loud, aggressive tone of voice. It's just fine to tell such people, "I can't deal with you when you're talking like that. Please calm down or else let's talk another time." If anyone is threatening bodily harm or actually lays hands on you in an angry gesture, you are perfectly within your rights to threaten to call the police. There is no excuse for any customer or client behaving abusively, no matter how disappointed they may be with your product or service.

A final tip: Treat your employees the way you want them to treat the customers. If you are not treating your employees well, that poor treatment will ultimately be reflected in how they treat your customers—and that will hurt your business.

Today's peacock is tomorrow's feather duster.

— Arthur Martinez, CEO, Sears

The only certain measure of success is to render more and better service than is expected of you.

— Og Mandino, author, **The Greatest Salesman in the World**

Do not do unto others as you would that they should do unto you. Their tastes may not be the same.

— George Bernard Shaw

Worry about getting better; bigger will take care of itself. Think one customer at a time and take care of each one the best way that you can.

— Gary Comer, founder, Lands' End

It is not the employer who pays wages—he only handles the money. It is the customer who pays the wages.

— Henry Ford

One of the most important lessons of business—the value of concentrating on the customers you have.

— Tom Monaghan, founder, Domino's Pizza

It is the service that we are not obliged to give that people value the most.

— James C. Penney

We consider our customers a part of our organization, and we want them to feel free to make any criticism they see fit in regard to our merchandise or service.

— L.L. Bean, founder, L.L. Bean Co.

Section VIII

MANAGEMENT

BUILD YOUR BUSINESS STRONGER—
AND DO IT QUICKLY!

Keeping Your People Happy

The simple act of paying positive attention to people
has a great deal to do with productivity.

— Thomas Peters and Robert Waterman, Jr.

Why was it you wanted to be on your own? For many
of you reading this, a prime reason was freedom. In other
words, you may not have taken all that well to being
"bossed around." So how are you going to "boss" your
own employees? Is there any danger that you may turn
into the kind of problem boss you were trying to get away
from? Shall we check it out and see?

After all, you've spent valuable time, energy, and money
hiring the best people you could find. This is because
you've read or heard about the studies that show that
high turnover is a killer. If you have to let people go, or if
people that you want to keep depart for greener pastures,
it will jeopardize the very life of your venture.

So how do you keep your workplace employee friendly?

Not simply by giving everybody a generous raise. Henry
Ford was fond of saying, "If we doubled every worker's
salary, it would improve the quality of the product very

little." That's because people want, yes, to be paid reasonably well. But they also want more than money.

People are also looking for a certain quality of life at work—a quality that you as a small business owner just may be able to provide better than larger and more impersonal corporations.

Small companies or units, such as yours, can often personalize training and work relationships, cross-train employees in many aspects of the firm, and develop a work atmosphere that feels more like belonging to a family.

Another advantage is that your employees can directly contribute to putting all the systems in place. Creative and energetic types love this. And they are the kind of people you will do well to hire and keep around.

Recognition Is Very Important

Recognition of employees' positive performance or ideas is also important. A study done by the U.S. Chamber of Commerce in 1986 asked both employees and their employers to rate what the employee wanted from his or her job. The results were surprising. The employees listed appreciation as number one, followed by "feeling in on things" and "help on personal problems." Their managers had listed these items as eighth, tenth, and ninth, respectively.

In other words, employees were looking for a reasonable quality of life, but managers were rather blind to that fact. A recent Department of Labor study revealed that 46 percent of those who quit their jobs did so because they felt unappreciated.

So make sure that your workplace is one where praise for an employee's worthwhile efforts is fully and generously expressed.

The One-Minute Manager, by Kenneth Blanchard,

Ph.D., and Spencer Johnson, M.D., offers this outline for acknowledging employees:

- Praise the behavior,
- do it soon,
- be specific,
- tell the person what they did right,
- and how you feel about it,
- encourage the person,
- shake hands.

When all is said and done, money does count. Do not delude yourself with the notion that you can pay bottom-of-the-barrel wages and get first-class people to come work for you and stay for the long haul. Pay as much as you can afford. For the rest, providing the quality of life we are talking about here will go a long way to compensate for any salary gap between your firm and the corporate giants, especially since, with wave after wave of downsizing, corporate America has become a very insecure place to earn a living.

Five Things to Avoid

There are certain other things that almost all employees dislike and that employers should avoid. Unfortunately, many of these things have become all too prevalent in stores, offices, and plants. Here are five:

1) Breaking Promises. A boss tells an employee, "Jack, you'll get a raise in six months if we reach our sales quota." The six months go by, the quota is reached, and guess what? The boss conveniently "forgets" about the promised raise. That puts Jack in the embarrassing position of having to go remind his boss and practically beg for what he'd been promised.

How can we avoid these very damaging breaches of trust with our employees?

There's an anonymous maxim that offers excellent advice in this regard: "Make few promises. Keep them all."

So do not promise things lightly. Think hard before you speak. Ask yourself, "What are the chances that I will be able to keep this promise?" Remember too that whatever you say to your employees will be taken as a promise. Be careful how you present things to them. If you want something to be taken as a firm promise, use the words, "I promise you." Otherwise, don't.

If you do find, despite all your best efforts, you have to renege on a promise, the only counsel I can give you is: Be very sensitive and apologetic and do your best to make good on the promise as soon as you possibly can.

Seek Your Employees' Input

2) Not Valuing Employees' Suggestions. Most people actually care about the business for which they work. They really do want you and your associates to succeed. Furthermore, they'd like to contribute to your success. To that end they will suggest things to you, such as changes to systems or ways of operating that can make them more effective or new products or services you might consider.

You can let your employees know that you take them seriously by actively soliciting their input. You can do this verbally, by memo, or by simply installing a suggestion box.

Even if you do not implement an employee suggestion, let them know you appreciated their making it. Employees who feel that you value their contributions are far more likely to stay with your firm.

A word of caution: If you are going to solicit suggestions, you must indeed implement some of the ones you receive. If you don't, your employees will become seriously frustrated and make you wish you had never asked for their ideas at all.

As to rewards, some companies provide a cash bonus for implemented suggestions. Others may offer an added day of vacation or some other attractive incentive. Small gifts often work well as a reward.

Good Communication Starts with You

3) Communicating poorly. Human beings like clarity and certainty. They absolutely abhor being kept in the dark about something that concerns their work life. For instance, employees may be unpleasantly surprised to discover that a new procedure is being installed in their work area. They'll want to know, "Why didn't you tell us this before?"

The solution to any communication problem has to start with you. You must take responsibility for any breakdown in communication—not blame—but responsibility. Even if an employee could rightly be blamed for not trying hard enough to understand, it's better if you tell everyone, "I guess I wasn't clear enough in trying to get that message across. Let me try it again."

When you have any doubt as to whether someone understood you, ask them: "Is that clear?" or "Would you like me to go over any item once again?" just as a good teacher would do.

Practice being straightforward and to the point. Shelve the distracting chit-chat, rambling stories, and long-winded explanations. And get rid of any need you may have to be right all the time. Sometimes you'll be wrong. Admit it, to yourself and to your employees. Above all, don't saddle them with blame for things that you yourself should have handled differently.

Remember also that men and women have somewhat different styles of communication. In general, men's first priority tends to be seeking information, while women tend to place their first priority on building relationships. Learn about the other gender's style and try to adapt to it.

Guidelines for Effective Reprimands

4) Mishandling reprimands. A classic no-no. Nothing leaves more of a permanent scar than poorly handled reprimands or critiques—unless it be getting fired without cause. This is the kind of thing an employee might never forget or forgive. Nobody, for example, enjoys working for a hothead who blows up at them in front of other employees.

Haven't you ever been in a store talking with a clerk and suddenly had a manager race out from a back office to berate the clerk for his or her latest mistake? Nor only did the clerk feel horrible; you, the customer, did too, right? The whole incident probably left you with a distinctly negative impression of not only the manager, but also the whole store.

Fortunately, this is the easiest gaffe to resolve. Do all reprimanding in private. This will greatly increase the likelihood that the employee will give you respectful attention, and he or she may resolve to modify behavior to fit your standards.

Once again, *The One-Minute Manager* has some excellent suggestions for you:
- Reprimand the behavior, not the individual.
- Do it as soon as possible after the problem occurs.
- Be specific.
- Tell the person what you believe they did wrong
- and also how you feel about it.

- Encourage the person.
- Shake hands.

I might add: Give the person a chance to offer an explanation. Perhaps your employee was ill or woozy from medication or exhausted from staying up all night with a feverish child. Perhaps the version of the mistake that you received from someone else was not entirely accurate. Then listen! If some aspect of the problem needs further investigation, promise that you'll do it or see that it gets done.

5) Giving one employee or another preferential treatment. This may well be the most damaging workplace habit of all. It says to your employees: Look, one or some of you are simply more important to me, the owner, than the rest of you, and those favored few can live by different rules (i.e., they can get off from work for personal errands more easily; they don't have to account fully for their work, especially their mistakes; they get to spend more "boss's pet" time with you, chatting or talking shop). Such employees have been put on a pedestal, and, believe me, their colleagues would like to bring them down from there with a fusillade of rocks.

Resentment will build fast in a workplace riven with preferential treatment. This in turn leads to gossip and snide comments: "There goes Mr. Better-than-us," or, "Little Miss Special Toes." Other appellations that may be whispered about could not be printed here.

The way around this is to apply the same workplace rules to everyone. Inevitably, you will have better "chemistry" with some employees than with others. You're human. Nonetheless, make sure that everyone knows that the rules are the rules, and all must abide by them or suffer the consequences.

The ability to deal with people is as purchasable a commodity as sugar and coffee. And I will pay more for that ability than for any other under the sun.

— John D. Rockefeller

The group will not prosper if the leader grabs the lion's share of the credit for the work that has been done.

— Lao-Tzu

How well we communicate is determined not by how well we say things but by how well we are understood.

— Andrew S. Grove, former CEO, Intel Corp.

The most important element in establishing a happy, prosperous atmosphere was an insistence upon open, free, and honest communications up and down the ranks of our management structure.

— Harold Geneen, former CEO, IT&T

I don't know about management techniques as such. I only know about engineering and people. The most important thing is the respect for people within the corporation, and so it's incumbent on the managers to create an environment within a corporation in which all employees are encouraged to take initiatives in carrying out the work, and doing the work with pleasure.

— Soichiro Honda, founder, Honda Motors

Sandwich every bit of criticism between two layers of praise.

— Mary Kay Ash

Resolving Conflicts at Work So Everybody Wins

The way we see the problem is the problem.

— Stephen R. Covey

A key supplier is late on a shipment—again! Because he is a real hothead, you dread calling to prompt him. But these late shipments of his have put a terrible strain on your business. So you call. He quickly gets offended and starts to yell at you over the phone. Forgetting your resolve to keep your cool, you start yelling back and finish in a huff. When you hang up, not only is your late shipment still left unresolved, but now you are angry and frustrated to boot. You spend the rest of the day spinning your wheels unproductively.

You like your partner, John, in the large retail outlet you have launched together. You enjoy having someone with whom to share the workload, and in general, your relationship is good. But periodically you get into knock-down, drag-out fights. The fights seem to come out of nowhere and are usually about some minor flap that could, you feel, be easily fixed if only you both could stay rational.

Your market research firm is small but dynamic. You have got some real scrappy people on board, and part of their energy flows into rivalries and quarrels. Despite your best intentions, you let yourself get drawn into these spats, too. "If only," you sigh after the umpteenth blowup between you and your staff, "we could talk things through without getting on each other's nerves!"

Is there any way out of such quagmires? How can you learn to talk to people such as the tardy supplier, the volatile partner, or the scrappy employees to improve your chances of getting your business needs met?

Most of us may be tempted to pull back, to reduce the dealings we have with people we consider "difficult." (And of course the irony is that these same folks often think that we are the difficult side of the equation.) Minimizing our interactions with others, however, is not the right road to better communications. Often, in fact, such pulling back only makes everything muddier, and it solves nothing.

The best model I have found yet for resolving such conflicts is called "Compassionate Communication," or "Nonviolent Communication." It was developed by Marshall B. Rosenberg, Ph.D., whose booklet, "A Model for Nonviolent Communication," describes the process. Rosenberg, who lectures around the USA and abroad, starts with the most common question in any culture. "How are you doing?" He ends up by showing you how to make a request to get the kind of response you need from the other person.

Rosenberg's model has four key steps, couched as questions:
1) What are you observing?
2) What are you feeling?
3) What are your unmet needs?
4) How can you frame a request to match your needs?

Observing

This first step may be harder than you may think. Most of us find it terribly wrenching to separate our observations from our interpretations of a given event.

Take the late shipment. What we know is happening is that the merchandise we need has not yet arrived. We also know that this has happened before. What we do not know is why the merchandise is late. Our interpretation may be that the supplier is slack or cannot keep promises or is just out to irritate us. Such interpretations, however, whether true or false, get in the way of our doing the observation step properly. Here we have to take our clue from the late great Jack Webb of Dragnet fame, "Just the facts, Ma'am." Often simply separating the facts from our interpretations will clarify things so much we will handle our dilemmas in much better fashion.

In this regard, I like a passage from a poem from Rosenberg's booklet that gives the difference between observing and reaction from the perspective of the person who is catching the flak:

I can handle your telling me
what I did or didn't do
And I can handle your interpretations
but, please don't mix the two.

If you want to confuse any issue
I can tell you how to do it:
Mix together what I do
with how you react to it.

Whenever we launch into attributing motives to someone or calling them an "idiot" or a "clown," we have stopped observing and are into interpreting. So don't do it.

Feeling

If we are out of touch with our feelings, we are out of touch with what we truly want. Feelings are messengers that tell us if our wants and needs are being met and if our values are being satisfied.

Consequently, we can greatly increase our productivity if we can learn to experience and express—in appropriate ways—our feelings and emotions. As a cultural whole, people in the United States are not very good with this—especially men. Most often we think it's "inappropriate" to express our feelings in a business context. But the truth is, we are not fully human until we give ourselves permission to express our feelings—and let others do the same in our presence.

The foremost emotion to emerge in many business relations, such as between partners, is, guess what? Anger! You come in one morning to find your partner has fired the part-time secretary, without consulting you. You are very upset over this because you knew the young woman had been breaking up with her boyfriend and was going through a tough week and that she promised to get her work back on track. Yes, you should express your anger, but not by accusing your partner of ignorance or hastiness or thoughtlessness.

Remember when sorting out your feelings to say "I feel . . ." (Whatever: hurt, disappointment, sad, angry, confused, frustrated . . .) You are not expressing a feeling when you say, "I feel you shouldn't have fired the secretary." What you are expressing is a thought or judgment.

If we manage to pinpoint our feeling in a given situation, we will be able to move on to Step Three in Rosenberg's model, describing our unmet needs or expectations. Feelings will point the way to such needs—always!

Expressing Needs

When we do not get what we want or need, we become unhappy and consequently less productive. So the first step toward being happy and productive is to know what we need and want (at work, at home, wherever). While this may seem patently obvious, many people just do not and cannot say what they want.

In the partnership example just cited, you needed to experience your partner as treating you as an equal in making important decisions. From your perspective, your partner has trampled all over your self-esteem. It is extremely important to identify something like this.

In pinpointing what you needed or wanted that was left unfulfilled, you have positioned yourself for taking the final step in the process of conflict resolution:

Making a Request

If it is true that the steps already discussed are usually not taken very well, or very consciously, this last step is rarely taken at all. Somehow we expect people around us to read our minds and simply deliver what we need without our ever asking or explaining to them what it is.

This is unrealistic. To get our needs accommodated, we must get into the habit of identifying them and putting them into the form of concrete, specific requests.

The more specific the request, the better. And try to frame the request in a positive form. One possible request to an associate might be, "Stop making decisions without consulting me." Much better would be to say, "Please include me in all major decisions." The second sentence will be better received and increases your chances of having your partner actually behave in the manner you desire. It is amazing how willing most people will be to help us, to meet us halfway, when we phrase our requests constructively. It is equally amazing how people will dig in and resist us when we demand things in an aggressive or accusing tone.

Be gentle with yourself in your efforts to apply Rosenberg's model. The techniques I have discussed here require patience. I have been aware of this model for more than a year now, and I have been attempting to use it for all this time. Even so, I have not mastered it. Far from it. When I am caught up in an upsetting situation, it feels like I go on automatic pilot. The model disappears, all the elements of the conflict get jumbled together, and I find myself mixing together in one nasty witch's brew, facts, emotions, interpretations, and judgments.

What works for me, and what I suggest for you, is to review the model regularly. And practice, practice, practice. Also, after each conflict to which you are a party, sit down with yourself afterward and do a post-mortem. Imagine yourself having applied the model well in a particular situation and ask yourself: What would I have done differently? Next time, try to do exactly that.

The only way to get the best of an argument is to avoid it.

— Dale Carnegie

People need a chance to see how much agreement is possible between seemingly intractable opponents.

— Robert Redford

We're all working together; that's the secret.

— Sam Walton

Try Out These Keys to Wisdom

How to Acquire Good Business Sense

We don't receive wisdom; we must discover it for ourselves
after a journey that no one can take for us or spare us.

— Marcel Proust

What can you affect? What is "out there" affecting you
and your enterprise that you cannot change but can only
react to? And how do you decide, in any given circum-
stance, what is the best course of action to follow—or even
whether you should take no action at all and let outside
forces take their course?

Thoughtful or productive answers to these questions
fall into the realm of "business wisdom."

Such wisdom often spells the difference between a business that slips into the doldrums and a business that
takes wing and soars. Every entrepreneur dreams of being able to make the right choices, fend off competitive
pressures, and grow his or her venture into something
dynamic—or at least viable for the long term.

Often referred to as "good business sense," business
wisdom is what helps owner-managers learn from what
goes right and what goes wrong. It is the ability to call up

many past experiences and then make decisions about a present situation so that the business gains customers, dollar volume, and profits.

Just how can we acquire this wisdom? Not strictly from spending a lifetime in business. With not very much trouble we could locate two individuals who have both spent thirty years in business, but whose results or assets look strikingly different. Tom may have started a TV and radio repair business two decades ago, but he made adjustments to take in computers, VCRs, fax machines, and complicated telephone systems and now is doing a terrific annual volume. His cousin Jake may have done something similar in a neighboring town, but kept himself limited to broadcast equipment. Clearly, Tom and Jake have made different choices. (Nonetheless, if Jake is actually content with a smaller business—never wanted the hassle of adding employees or accounts and is making ends meet—perhaps that's enough for *him*.)

If wisdom then cannot be equated with experience, what is it?

Separate Facts from Opinions

At its base, business wisdom really consists of the ability to distinguish between facts and opinions and to create powerful interpretations of a set of facts. What we're aiming for is achieving a certain viewpoint that will open up options that will lead to desirable results, rather than getting hemmed in by limiting our actions or by taking no action at all.

The first step is to distinguish fact from opinion. It is a fact at E-Z Market Research that gross revenues rose by 14 percent in the second quarter and fell back by 7 percent in the third quarter. However, the apparent causes for the rise and fall may be merely hypotheses (such as the addition of a dynamic salesperson the previous March and the usual summer slump in July and August). While interpretations of the sales chart may be subjective, such interpretations are nonetheless extremely important.

Initially, you may ask, "What is a good interpretation as opposed to a bad interpretation?" Right here, let me stop you. The question itself is misleading because it is posed as "good" vs. "bad." Good vs. bad is not the best way to evaluate your interpretations because, calling upon Aristotelian logic, it implies that one decision is "all good," while another is "all bad." Life, like business, is rarely 100 percent "right" choices or 100 percent "wrong" choices. We find ourselves, more often than not, dealing in shades of gray. A more useful question is the following: "Which interpretation of the facts will help us reach our goals more quickly and easily?"

Four Steps to Improve Wisdom

Here are four steps to improve the way you interpret a set of facts (and, consequently, the way you acquire keener business wisdom):

1. Decide when you are dealing with a fact and when you are dealing with an interpretation. Separate the two! Facts are facts. They are set in stone. Nothing you can do will change the reality of a fact, such as an enormous discount bookstore moving into a town where your independent book mart had previously been the big fish in the pond.

Most of us have gotten into the unfortunate habit of mixing facts and opinions together. But here's a clue: Facts can be measured and counted. They are physical. They can be seen or heard. Facts include the month's sales volume, response rates for an ad campaign, and what a vendor said in a letter explaining shipping costs.

Interpretations, on the other hand, are not physical. They cannot be seen or heard. They are your thoughts, beliefs, or opinions about something. Many times, interpretations respond to the question, "What does this fact (or set of facts) mean?" Interpretations include hypothesized reasons why sales volume was so high (or so low), what went wrong with the ad campaign, and what the vendor really meant (reading between the lines) in her letter.

2. Hone or fine-tune your interpretations to bring them in closer alignment with reality (what actually is). This is something you can rarely do alone. Checking your interpretation with the interpretations of others helps immensely. Perhaps you are too willing to blame the third-quarter drop on the dog days of summer, while someone on your staff has noticed some non-seasonal factor, such as a weak advertising campaign that may explain some of the slump. Dialoguing or brainstorming with staff or others may also expose hidden factors that will sharpen your interpretation. Concerted research into certain situations will also help.

See Many Different Perspectives

3. Acquire the ability to see things from a number of different perspectives (that is, not just your own). This is to survey a set of facts and not only realize that you are interpreting them, but also that a variety of interpretations is possible—and then actually to seek out interpretations different from your own. These may come from a partner, staff, your accountant, lawyer or banker, or family and friends.

The ability to see a situation from a number of different viewpoints is extremely valuable in business; in fact, this ability may even be decisive in whether or not your venture ever grows to match your visions or dreams.

In a business that has grown into having people staffing different departments, there will be department-based views that will naturally evolve. *Pay attention to each one!* Each has value. Accounting will always focus on cost factors related to a decision or ongoing action. Marketing will want to look at possible rewards or returns, often in a hypothetical way. Operations will notice changes that have to be implemented to add a feature to a product. Sales will bear down on how this new feature will add value to the product and give the reps more sales ammunition. And if your business is not of the size to have departments as yet, you and your associates must put on different hats and try to represent these different perspectives yourselves. Coaches or outside consultants (and these may be your CPA or your banker) can definitely help.

Learning to appreciate different perspectives will also teach you the value of diversity. You will be better equipped to notice how people from different cultural backgrounds or different ages may see things in different ways. And each way of seeing offers some advantages for growing your business.

I do not, however, mean to imply that all viewpoints are equally beneficial. Some, clearly, will be more useful than others for moving your operation ahead. Your job as owner-manager is to welcome all viewpoints in the first instance, then select those that hold the most promise for productive change and put them into action.

See the Relatedness of Events

4. See the relatedness of events and decisions. In other

words, cultivate systems thinking. In your business—and in the marketplace—many things are interrelated. Briefly, decisions in one domain affect decisions in others. What gets decided and put into action in marketing will have an impact on operations, sales, and human resources. Decisions made in a strategic planning session will affect production and sales. Notice this phenomenon and take it into account as you go about translating decisions into policy and action.

Being able to see and appreciate the interrelatedness of all aspects of your business and all aspects of the market niche in which you operate will set you apart. This is a brand of business wisdom that, in my experience, few people possess. So arm yourself with this and the other three skills I've sketched for you, and move up toward that peak of success you can already glimpse, shimmering in the clouds high above.

What lies ahead of you and what lies behind of you is nothing compared to what lies within you.

— Mohandas Gandhi

The teacher, if indeed wise, does not bid you to enter the house of their wisdom, but leads you to the threshold of your own mind.

— Kahlil Gibran

Knowledge comes, but wisdom lingers.

— Alfred Lord Tennyson